WHAT IF WE CONSIDERED motherhood an organizing principle instead of a genre or subject?

In her debut book of essays, Chantal Braganza explores what we reach for as we search for our family's place in the world. Can we believe the people who have given us the story of who we are? And how do we craft that story for our own children when we're still struggling to describe ourselves?

Considering the limits of understanding motherhood as an identity or action alone, Branganza reflects on her upbringing as a daughter of Mexican and Indian immigrants, the first years of raising her two children, and the physicality of motherhood and loss, nourishment and violence.

Weaving dreamlike memoir sections of her childhood—myths and memories passed down from Vallarta, Mombasa, London, and Toronto—with urgent essays about migration, identity, and speech, *Story of Your Mother* wrangles with the restraints of language, finding that even fluency doesn't guarantee the ability to translate words into meaning for your children.

Can we believe the people who have given us the story of who we are? And how do we craft that story for our own children?

Praise for
Story of Your Mother

"Prismatic, poignant, and resilient. Chantal Braganza seamlessly extrapolates motherhood as identity, action, and definition. *Story of Your Mother* is a bewitching debut."
—Scaachi Koul, author of *Sucker Punch*

"An intimate collage of memory, culture, and family history; an eloquent meditation on the multitudes of selfdom. Braganza explores motherhood not as a universal experience, but as a structure open to boundless interpretation."
—Desmond Cole, author of *The Skin We're In: A Year of Black Resistance and Power*

"In *Story of Your Mother*, Chantal Braganza manages the extraordinary. This is a book that fuses profound and tender meditations on care with a potent and edifying insistence that its invisible politics be made visible. Braganza expertly renders poignant scenes of motherhood, then turns them into portals to urgent questions about family, migration, labour, and colonialism. This is a rich book, poetic and expansive, clear-eyed in its aim: Braganza inverts the question—what if motherhood wasn't the fixed thing to be examined, but the lens itself? *Story of Your Mother* deepens our vocabulary of motherhood by showing us connections that have always been there, right in front of us, the whole time."
—Elamin Abdelmahmoud, host of CBC's *Commotion*

"A stunning meditation on motherhood, identity and inheritance. Chantal blends personal history with incisive cultural critique seamlessly in prose that is both tender and profound. It's an exceptionally empathetic work that is also incredibly honest. Chantal has written a deeply moving memoir that I'll think about for years to come."

—Sadiya Ansari, author of *In Exile*

"Sharp and smart and unsentimental—but full, packed to the brim, with a million different shades of love—Chantal Braganza's *Story of Your Mother* brings together beginnings and endings, migrations and returns, food and family and history and colonialism, pregnancy and birth and mothering and labour, all in a story that flows like rivers seeking the same terminal sea."

—andrea bennett, author of *Hearty*

Story of Your Mother

Story of
Your
Mother

Chantal Braganza

STRANGE
LIGHT

Strange Light is a registered trademark of Penguin Random House Canada Limited.

The authorized representative in the EU for product safety and compliance is Penguin Random House Ireland, Morrison Chambers, 32 Nassau Street, Dublin D02 YH68, Ireland, https://eu-contact.penguin.ie

Library and Archives Canada Cataloguing in Publication
Title: Story of your mother / Chantal Braganza.
Names: Braganza, Chantal, author.
Identifiers: Canadiana (print) 20240432088 | Canadiana (ebook) 20240432134
    | ISBN 9780771009686 (hardcover) | ISBN 9780771009693 (EPUB)
Subjects: LCSH: Braganza, Chantal. | LCSH: Motherhood. | LCSH:
    Women—Identity. | LCGFT: Autobiographies.
Classification: LCC HQ759 .B73 2025 | DDC 306.874/3092—dc23

Cover design: Jennifer Griffiths
Typeset in Legacy Serif ITC Pro by Erin Cooper
Printed in the United States of America

Published by Strange Light,
an imprint of Penguin Random House Canada,
320 Front Street West, Suite 1400
Toronto, Ontario, M5V 3B6, Canada
penguinrandomhouse.ca

1st Printing

Penguin
Random House
Canada

The way I became a writer was that my mother wrote my life for me and told it to me.

— JAMAICA KINCAID

The point, or part of it, is that babies eat manuscripts. They really do. The poem not written because the baby cried, the novel put aside because of a pregnancy, and so on. Babies eat books. But they spit out wads of them that can be taped back together.

— URSULA K. LE GUIN

A BABY IS BORN IN reverse. Transverse, as the medical literature defines it, or bum-first, as his mother will remind him well into his adult years and especially after he has children of his own. So painful, and so many hours! For this, or perhaps other reasons, he never lives it down.

He grows up the third child of four, and walks to school most mornings. One day he will tell his children about the giraffes and cheetahs and other animals he sees on these walks, perhaps because this is what he thinks they are taught about Mombasa, where he grew up. In truth the roads are lined with concrete block homes and bare of animals, the schools segregated by religion and race. He is well into his teens before he sees a giraffe for the first time, and even then it is from a train.

He is sent to boarding school in Goa, western India, from where his family originates. This is at significant expense to his father, who fixes beaten-up instruments, recycles Christmas presents, and bakes cakes for tuition money. It is meant as a gift, a prized education. But the young man hates the 5 a.m. wakings and knuckle-beatings and other punishments he still doesn't have language for, so much so that he begs in letters to leave. He threatens to kill himself. When his father relents, the boy heads straight to London to join his older brother, who once endured the same gift himself.

The boy is seventeen. He is fond of flared pants and oil paints and Marvel comics and is so delirious with this new version of his life that he visits the same pub a block from his flat frequently enough to imagine himself working there.

He feels free; free in a place that once claimed strict ownership of the other places he has lived in and is supposed to be from.

Three years later, his father dies of a stroke. His sister writes from Toronto to deliver the news.

A small girl is hit by a car. She is the last of six children, and born tiny. Perhaps she is hard to see, or simply unused to the cobblestone roads; her family has moved from a mountain town in western Mexico to a beach-resort city where her father hopes to start a practice as a lawyer. She is thrown a few feet by the impact. Her nose is broken and rearranged. Her grandmother sees this from the child's bedroom window; the same one she looks up at to watch her granddaughter jumping up and down on her bed. She rushes out to the child.

Years later, when her daughter asks her about her own nose, bent awkwardly in that growth spurt between small childhood and something slightly older, the woman points to her own face, where the break still shows, and tells this story. It's meant to be a shared experience, but the girl understands it as a causal explanation. That wounds, and the way they heal, are inherited.

She also tells stories about water. About the Cuale River, which cleaves the beachside city on its way to the ocean, opaque and still and not fit for swimming but often used for laundry and bankside gossip. When she was sixteen, a particularly violent hurricane ripped up houses along the Cuale and emptied their contents into the angry, swollen water. The next morning she and her sisters ran to the riverbank to watch. Clay shingles, refrigerators, electric fans swirling into the Pacific. The storm hadn't ended yet, and they shouldn't have been there. She should have been afraid.

A man delivers chicken for a restaurant chain in the evenings, and reports on the size of property lots in the daytimes for the City of Toronto. By day he is treated with respect, but something happens in the evenings, something not unexpected but still life-changing in his experience of the world afterwards. He is more aware than ever of his status of not being born to a place, of non-inheritance, of seeking varying levels of either approval or respect from people who can be at turns patronizing, kind, or cruel for reasons that have more to do with their own discomfort with the feelings his presence gives rise to than anything he's actually done.

But his mother, brothers, and sisters are living in the same city, together again after nearly a decade in different places across the globe. He has good friends. A job that will allow him a sabbatical to travel. He's delivering chicken; he's saving money. He's headed to Greece in a month and he can't believe his luck.

A young woman, newly seventeen, starts a job as a server at a beachside restaurant called Las Palomitas. She is headed to university next year, needs the money, and the clientele along the boardwalk simply tip better. For a time the town's cobblestone streets were known as a hideout for movie stars, somewhere Richard Burton could build a pleasure palace for Elizabeth Taylor or Sylvester Stallone could party in relative peace. The tourists who followed brought cash and spent heavily.

Before the town's beaches were segregated by private hotels, men in printed button-ups, cooked vermilion by the sun, would squelch out kissing sounds at her. One evening, one of these lobster men follows her around the restaurant while she is on shift, sketching her likeness. It's accurate and very beautiful. Part tip, part gesture. She will keep the portrait stuffed away in her closet somewhere.

Six months into this venture, a man walks into the bar. He has just flown in from Athens and is hopelessly clueless about this destination because he is not meant to be here; an earlier plan to island-hop in Greece was cut short when he met a couple in Mykonos who beckoned him to Puerto Vallarta, a multi-layover, nearly thirty-hour trip in the opposite direction. He cannot speak a word of the language. But he tries.

Two years later, she leaves her family and boards a flight to Toronto.

After the wedding, after the flight, after the scramble for a place to live, the couple moves into a studio condominium in Port Credit, a micro-suburb by the water of a nearby lake. This mirrors some aspects of their meeting. Another beachside town.

Another mirror: when money gets tight, they both find side gigs in food service whenever and wherever they can. Once, together, at a hotel restaurant in this lakefront community. He plays the bartender; she works as a server. Guests flock to her.

He doesn't know how to make a screwdriver. He is fired in the first week.

I DON'T REMEMBER EVER asking my parents where it was I came from, or from whom. The answers were relayed to me often and built into the fabric of everyday life. I came home from school; my grandmother made fideos. I spoke a different language then, saw extended family regularly then, was often asked this question at school, and asked it of my friends in return. In the eighties and early nineties Mississauga was only in its teens, and much of its population growth was driven by immigration. In every elementary school classroom, dine-in Pizza Hut, shopping mall corridor; the only majority reflected in these neighbourhoods was that most people were, generationally recently, *from somewhere*. My life reflected no other reality until I left the city to work as a journalist in Toronto. The specific confluence of those three factors—*work, journalist, Toronto*—changed my environment significantly. Far fewer of the people I came to meet or work with were *from somewhere*, unless that place was a town, a city, a school.

I can tell you this to illustrate how little I knew about the rest of what's called Canada; how, if born elsewhere in the country, I may early on have been more likely to identify myself through a lens of absence, of non-whiteness. I can tell you this to illustrate how lucky I was not to, which is true. But these demographic realities themselves—that we could all be *from* somewhere, that we were all from somewhere *together* in a way incongruent with the rest of the country—only demonstrate the work of colonialism and white supremacy in negative relief, an inverse shape.

I can tell you this to emphasize that I grew up understanding that race is an empirical fact, yes, but that I had not yet been explicitly encouraged to consider its social and historical grammar. *My father is from Kenya, but he's Goan, which means he's Indian.* (The syntax in that statement!) *My mother is Mexican.* (The implied simplicity!) I did not have to ask my parents where I was from, but I was asked it often enough to become comfortable answering the question in whichever way suited the context.

I can tell you this one day, when you haven't asked, precisely because you aren't likely to. I often think about the ways your life may have indirectly answered the question for you already.

THERE ARE SOME BIOLOGICAL theories that, at times, feel like the right description of what it felt like to carry a child.

Not the feeling of being pregnant, not seeing the same curvature of the shell of your ear in your child's. I mean literal cellular invasion; genetic material that passes from the fetus, through the placenta, into the tissues throughout the body; brain, liver, bones, blood; cells believed at once to have a protective effect and to be potentially harmful. Some studies have shown fetal cells rush to the site of a heart injury. Others suggest they may play a role in influencing autoimmune disorders. They live on in the body for years after birth, sometimes decades, a kind of parting gift. I don't know where my children's cells live on in me. But I know they're there.

I also know that pregnancy isn't the only way mothers, parents, families are made—and that relying only on the kinds of stories we build around biology can be as misleading as it is harmful.

Let me try again.

Think of a short, propositional phrase. Something true. *Water is clear. Blood is red.* In the case of my children, while I carried them: *I am you.* At the time, there was no distinction. I made the decision that there was, in fact, an indivisible us—not just me, not me *and* baby, not a fetus with rights that superseded mine—an ontological power too many people invested in consolidating power would rather not exist.

For a short while you were more *of* me, and every single day of my pregnancies I chose this—even while learning through each experience just how little control this choice actually imparts in comparison to the caprice of the body.

I made this decision years before I fully understood why it was the right one. Part of this understanding includes the fact that the distinction of knowing why or not in the moment of the decision's making doesn't quite matter, so much as the continued willingness to engage with the question long after the fact. Perhaps for the rest of one's life? I want to find out.

Now: make that proposition relational. *Water has clearness. Blood has a redness.* And in the case of my children: *I have you.* Or rather: *I have a youness to me.* It is only the English language's reliance on the concept of ownership to demonstrate relationships that makes this sound like an exercise in possession. What I am talking about is that giving birth to and caring for my children wasn't a reproduction, but a transformation—into a relationship, yes, but also of transformed relationships with everything and everyone else.

In some disciplines, this is known as hypostatic abstraction. In math, all predicates that take more than one object become relational. In linguistics, more than one thing becomes the subject; what is being discussed no longer exists in a hierarchy. It needn't be one-directional, the same way there is no one direction through which a child comes into someone's life, or a parent into a child's.

Sometimes I think about Elena Ferrante's Lenù, and the last time she embraces her mother: "It was as if she meant to slip inside me and stay there, as once I had been inside her." About Jacqueline Rose, napping contentedly one afternoon shortly after she has come out on the other side of the adoption process and her infant daughter is home. She wakes up in a panic: did she fall asleep with her child lying on top of her? No, her child has found a place inside her, "an inverse pregnancy, moving backwards in time," her daughter claiming space in her bloodstream as Rose is "turned inside out."

Meanwhile, the baby has in fact been sleeping in her crib the whole time—a waking trick of the mind that will be familiar to anyone who has lived through the sleep deprivation of early parenthood. It takes her a moment to realize what she is feeling is joy, unfettered and destabilizing. "Had anyone told me in advance this was an experience common to adopting mothers . . . I have no doubt I would have lain awake waiting, fruitlessly, for it to happen."

Complete dispossession; the self is shattered, waiting to be rearranged. However it happens, whatever the order, we become each other, and after it we are never the same. If we are lucky, on and on it goes; there is no origin.

THE IDEA OF AN origin had a romance to it before you were born. When I was your age, it was the easiest language I had with both of your grandparents. Stories about where they came from, and therefore stories about where I came from; a series of steps originating from two points on nearly opposite sides of the globe and landing in a little three-bedroom house at the edge of a brand-new suburban development west of Toronto. An explanation for our presence there, an unquestioned talisman. *I was born somewhere else. Life there was good, but difficult. I came here, where life was good, but difficult in other ways. I worked hard. This place kept its promise to me.*

Everyone among us has an origin story of some kind, though not everyone among us is encouraged to talk about it honestly as part of the social fabric of what we call Canada; an unspoken price of belonging to a place that relies on such stories in order to become real in a way that does not betray its own parasitic history.

"Too much has been made of origins," writes Dionne Brand. "All origins are arbitrary. This is not to say that they are not also nurturing, but they are essentially coercive and indifferent."

A few years ago, I told you an offhand story about how your grandfather delivered Swiss Chalet meals as an evening job in his first years living in Toronto. It was the fourth lockdown of the pandemic, and when we ordered our Friday pizza treat, the courier would leave it in a sticker-sealed box at the foot of our door. When you finally saw Pa again, you asked him if he was still a "pizza man." I was not prepared for how much this would bother him.

Not because he felt it in any way embarrassing or undignified, but because, despite telling me his own versions of origin stories for years, it was the first time he had been materially presented with the fact that such tellings could be relayed differently, understood in a way he did not expect—that they took on a life of their own after they were given. Specifically, it was the first time he had been presented with the fact that the stories he told could be passed down more than once, repurposed, the idea of beginnings diluted and debunked.

You were barely four at the time, and it's unlikely that much of what either of us wanted to say would have stayed with you in the way we intended. I wanted to tell you a story that contextualized your family in the world around you as it was in the moment; he wanted it made clear that this part-time job was one step in a series of events that led to him meeting your grandmother, part of his own codified origins in a place called Canada. The world I was translating for you—your world—would shrink and expand wildly those first two years of the plague, in ways I hadn't experienced as a child and, as a parent, constantly questioned how to navigate with care. One origin glossed in amber, another told out of fear. Instead, you heard these words, translated and once-removed; you thought, *pizza!* One story, told three times over, each of them a little true.

Coercive and indifferent. Is it coercive to talk to you about these things, to address you in this way? When I worry about this, I try to remember a sentiment repeated to me more than once when family and friends first met you: *Wow, two days in labour? Just wait till you get to bring this up when they're a teenager.* Those hours I spent in bathtubs, on yoga balls, or keeled over in the shower are no longer memorable or particularly important to me. I tried, for a few months afterwards, to codify them in some way—to narrativize and attach meaning. I thought that the fact of birth itself, that those hours, marked the passage to motherhood. Weren't they part of an origin story? Didn't they mean something? What would you want to know about them someday?

I am not interested in using that anecdote as a parenting technique, ever; nor do I see it as a feat of strength these days. What I needed was medical intervention. I was up until that point too invested in the idea of an empowering birth—convinced that such a thing was guaranteed to those who knew what they were doing, convinced that such a thing was even possible when it came to giving birth for the first time—that I waited entirely too long to insist upon going to the hospital and getting an epidural. I endured the pain because I was afraid of giving up control. That isn't strength. I've learned and relearned that lesson often since, which I think gets closer at what a passage looks like.

What did I gain by waiting? I have trouble remembering so much about that labour, perhaps because an extended expectation like that removed my attention to detail. Sometimes this bothers me, and sometimes I think about the only two concrete things I know of the story of my own birth, repeated to me by your grandparents. From my mother: that I was born on a warm day, sunny, after twenty-four hours of labouring alone, walking through hospital wards where she heard other women shrieking. And from my father, when he calls to remind me each year: the minute I was born, Cutting Crew's "(I Just) Died in Your Arms" was playing on the radio.

At one point, maybe hour twelve, the midwife recommended I rent a TENS machine that would rhythmically send electrical shocks through wires and stickers into my lower back to help me endure the pain. It's easy to laugh about it now, this image of your father timidly pushing buttons on a stupid little black box in between bouts of me heaving what felt like gallons of yellow bile into the toilet. It felt horrible, trying to solve the problem of pain with more of the same. *What a way to enter the world*, I thought. I had been working on a baby quilt for you throughout my entire pregnancy that I regretted not finishing. It took thirty-two hours for me to ask for the drugs; it would be another ten till I held you.

When I gave birth to your brother, I had exactly the birth I thought I wanted. I woke up to contractions, called the midwife, packed for the hospital, and was hooked up to painkillers within hours. I even put on a face mask while getting dressed. It wasn't seamless: I bled everywhere, my arms wouldn't keep a needle, and at one point the umbilical cord snapped at the root of the placenta with a sickening wet *pop!*, momentarily leaving the ephemeral organ lost inside me after birth. The midwife frantically used both hands to get it out. But compared to the endless hours, it was deliciously, frighteningly calm.

In experiencing the grace of that rare cooperation of the body, its environment, and a medical system that tries to mediate both, I came to believe that the first time, I had robbed myself of the agency I wanted by denying myself help for so long. I know now that both times I was looking for agency through two different versions of control.

The second time around, experience had taught me what I wanted and what to ask for. This is a type of power, no doubt. But knowledge cannot guarantee knowledge of the outcome, and it cannot always give you what you want. I wanted the story of a "good" birth. I'm no longer sure there is such a thing.

I have talked with you about being born before, but I saved this part. I want to be honest, because even though it may not touch you in your life the way it did me, it will always accompany you—the way death does, too. Birth can be beautiful, yes, but it can also be chaotic and impossible to categorize. There is no natural or unnatural, moral or immoral version of the experience, and so much harm stems from our attempts to impress these specific narratives on it. Birth can be beautiful, and often it is. But if not coercive, it, too, can be indifferent.

I understand now that the sacred parts, for me, began with an image: New Year's Day, only it was evening by then. The midwife held you up in the hospital light, made syrupy by the drugs I'd finally taken. Your mouth open, a soundless howl of shock and surprise. I saw you before I heard you, and that image is with me still.

"BOOKS LEAVE GESTURES IN the body; a certain way of moving, of turning, a certain closing of the eyes, a way of leaving, hesitations," Dionne Brand writes in *A Map to the Door of No Return*, a book you have often seen me holding, that I have returned to many times lately, that your brother has scribbled little loops in, perhaps mimicking gestures of my own.

She describes reading *The Black Napoleon* and *Lady Chatterley's Lover* for the first time, experiences both agonizing ("I did not yet know how the world took people like me") and ecstatic (she "emerged having reconstructed the novel into a more complex, more fluid sense of desire"). "I suspect that I have been writing these two books ever since, recalling and reimagining them," she writes.

A foundational text is a type of origin. So are its redactions, deletions, its active thefts. *A Map* begins with a question her grandfather feels he knows intimately but cannot easily answer: "What people we came from." She asks it repeatedly, growing up at the southernmost tip of Trinidad, on the precipice of the span of the Atlantic. The lack of an answer reveals "a rupture in history, a rupture in the quality of being." It disturbs her, propels her, draws a line to the door she writes of—the point of forced departure, the violent removal of history, one origin for the global Black diaspora. I reread this book on our couch, in airplane seats, in hotel lobbies while waiting to check in.

How little I had in common with this context; how much language Brand's writing gave me despite this. Proof that I did not have to always seek mirror reflections of myself to understand myself better, and a gentle prompt to look at and move in the world around me with care. Brand's writing reordered how I think about origins and belonging, and reaffirmed something often relayed to me about creation.

Many of us involved in the act of creation, of many kinds, will retell and refine one story over and over our entire lives, in different ways, in the process making it the story *of* our lives. I don't think this diminishes the pursuit; I think it can lead to clarity. Retelling can be coerced, habitual, generationally traumatic. In the hands of someone concerned with its stewardship, it can also be purposeful, intentionally transgressive.

Perhaps I should have told you Pa's takeout delivery story with a different sense of purpose.

I HAVE BEEN THINKING about return as a form of reproduction. One story, told many times over, each one a little true.

ONCE UPON A TIME, a princess named Mirra was born in a beautiful city, a wealthy place with pale buildings made of sparkling white marble, freshly cut.

Where?

Agra, where the Taj Mahal was built.

Have you seen it?

No.

Was she pretty?

She was, very. She wore ribbons sewn into her skirt, and ribbons in her hair. One day, a band of pirates saw her ribbons and fine dress, and sneaked into the white-stone city to kidnap her for sale.

Where was she from?

India, bunch. Let me tell the story. The pirates were from far away, and planned to bring her back to Portugal, where they were from.

You're from Portugal!

No, I'm from Kenya. Nana speaks Portuguese because

Goa was part of Portugal once. Can I finish the story please?

Okay, Daddy.

The princess was too smart for the pirates, who were misers and drunks and ended up taking her to the Philippines instead. She slipped out of their shackles and ran away to a Jesuit convent. The nuns were so delighted with her ribbons and beauty that they took her in, blessed her, and gave her a new name: Catarina de San Juan.

But Catarina es un Spanish name!

The Philippines were once owned by Spain, bunchkin.

Oh, okay.

Catarina strolled the streets of her new home in Manila. She got used to her new life, without caste or religion. But she always kept her ribboned hair and robes, and she grew ever more beautiful by the day. One day the pirates, still sulking from losing her, found her and stole her away again.

Again?

Yes—again! And this time, they took her farther away, to New Spain—

They took her where?

It's Mexico, bunch. Or actually, Latin Amer—

Why?

Because it once belonged to Spain, too.

Why?

I'll tell you later. Let me tell this story first. In New Spain, the pirates intended to sell her into service to a king, who had heard of her beauty and ribbons. He promised to pay a handsome price for the girl. But once the pirates had landed, rumours of her spread so quickly that people began to bid on her until one man, a merchant, outbid them all with offers of gold and silver and rubies and emeralds and sapphires—obscene treasures. He brought Catarina to his home, where he and his wife treated her the way they thought a child—which they had always wanted but never had—should be treated. Every day, a new dress and a new set of ribbons. The women of Puebla—

Of where?

Puebla, near Mexico City. You've been there. The women of the city loved her ribbons so much that they began to dress the same way: sewn into their skirts, woven into their hair. They called her La China Poblana, the Indian Princess of Mexico.

China means India?

That's . . . that's not what *china* means in Spanish.

What does it mean?

I'll tell you tomorrow. Go to sleep.

THE FIRST TIME THE woman brings her daughter back home, the baby is four months old and she is twenty-five, still young enough to instinctively call the coastwise town "back home" both in language and in thought.

And it's true, though home often must come to her. Her mother flies to Toronto to accompany her through the first few weeks of motherhood—a sleepless, stupid carousel only her older siblings have had the benefit of seeing before. When her milk doesn't come and the baby gets sick and skinny, her mother is there. When there has been no sleep for days, her mother is there. When her husband has returned to work and she's driving in circles two weeks after her daughter is born, trying to find the church where her niece will be baptized, her mother is there.

When her mother is there, there is plenty of time, of care. It doesn't last long, but for as long as they can afford it, it's enough.

So when the baby is older and there is enough money,

the woman is excited. She gets on a plane before her husband does. She packs suitcases of all-white outfits, diapers, gifts of makeup and clothes. Her daughter speaks a few words, another gift. She cannot wait to see the water again.

They arrive in August, the hottest month. The baby sweats and complains and grows big, angry boils on her nose and forehead. She is still teething and screams most of the way. It is almost as if she does not want to be there.

IN DICTIONARY SPANISH, *CONCHITA* means "little shell," a diminutive of the larger object, a concha. In many Spanish-speaking parts of the world, *concha* doubles as shape-descriptive slang for a vulva. In Mexico, it is also a sweet thing—a cottony breakfast roll coated in a thin sugar skin. Since size descriptions and endearments often work the same way in the language, much meaning is rolled into this word. They are shells, sex, bread, and, for plenty of Latin Americans, a food memory. Another type of madeleine.

Conchita is the nickname of my aunt Concepción, a woman who has taught me more about how to eat than most anyone else. These are her rules: if you can cook for others, do it; eat fruit every day; if you can soak it in milk, you should. I saw her more often when I was a girl, when my mother would bring my brother and me back to Mexico to visit her side of the family for holidays. These were the years Conchita wore creamy hot pink lipsticks, would tease my bangs into little poufs with hairspray, and ran a shop in front of the family home in Puerto Vallarta that sold diapers and stationery and gum. It was the size of a double garage. Or half of that, as my uncle Guillermo ran his carnicería out of the same space, a single row of refrigerated beef cuts he'd further slice down for customers with a square steel knife. He slipped my cousins, my brother, and me small bills from his wooden cash register. We marched them across the shop floor to buy candy.

In the mornings, a truck would arrive with cow parts to be unloaded into the store's back freezer and a boy would bike over conchas for the shop to sell, the basket of sweet bread balanced on his head. In the afternoons I'd walk up and down the aisles sucking Coca-Cola out of a plastic fruit bag with a straw. My aunt quizzed me on English words and held cans of chilled Fanta to her cheeks and throat. Those summers were unforgivingly hot, but every morning without fail there were conchas, papaya, and hot coffee for breakfast. I'd pick the cinnamon-flecked sugar skins off the rolls before pouring coffee-spiked milk over large pieces of the bread. I still do this with any baked thing, though the liquid needn't always be milk. My husband's Italian grandmothers taught me to soak bread in red wine, and cake in white.

Conchita has only disciplined me twice in my life. First, when I was five and threw a headless Barbie doll my cousin and I were fighting over into a pot of pozole she was making for company. The second time was a couple of years later, when she was making better money selling palm-sized tacos filled with grilled head and tongue meat to drunk tourists downtown. One evening a woman walked into the smoky little taquería, and I shamelessly gaped at her the entire time she ate. I'd never been to the Zona Romántica before, knew nothing of drag, did not know how to act. Her hair was huge, a miracle. She wore a beard and bright red lips. Her shoes were silver leather, ones I'd seen in a shop a few blocks away. She had to duck to get through the entrance of the restaurant.

"Chantal, cómo se dice dios en inglés?" Conchita hissed at me after the woman left. *How do you say God in English?* I answered, not understanding the question.

"Well, in the eyes of God that woman is a person, and you've just ruined her dinner." She reapplied the makeup the grill had steamed off and got back to work.

Because my abuelo didn't speak much when I knew him, I remember him mostly through objects, and stories about them. There were the deliveries—mornings my mother and her siblings would wake up to a truckload of watermelons, or this one time thirty caged parrots, which my abuelo had accepted as payment for legal representation despite having six children to clothe and feed. There was the silver tray on which he'd take his breakfast on the mornings when he was too weak to get up: conchas and Nescafé instant coffee, milk on the side. There was the case of 1980 Dom Pérignon he saved up for and brought to my mother's wedding, which one of the caterers stole.

There was the blue nylon trucker hat he wore through most of the nineties, which he'd use on occasion to spank his grandchildren. That same visit as the Barbie doll, I convinced all of my younger cousins to tear apart a morning delivery of conchas, thinking that they would sell better if we made them into new shapes. We kneaded the shell-shaped pastries into sticks, circles, and triangles, as if they were pizza dough, leaving sticky pink and white crumbs all over the red linoleum floor. We all got the blue hat for that one, even though it was only my fault. "Your aunt works [*smack*] so [*smack*] hard [*smack*]," he said. I ran to tell my mother, and didn't touch the shop's pastries for the remainder of the visit. For a very long time, I regretted both things.

I remember feeling I'd contributed to an ongoing splintering between my mother's life in Mexico and life in what eventually solidified its status as home. Growing up in Canada, my brother and I were never spanked. As young children, we went to Mexico often, sometimes for months at a time. Life in one place seemed like life in any other, and differences took upon meaning-making work. I interpreted them specifically, the way a child would, and that tendency stayed with me for a long time.

Pan dulce weren't a common find in suburban Toronto at the time, and were not particularly quick to make. The first time I tried to make conchas, I over-kneaded the dough and ruined the craquelin-esque sugar skin. They came out chewy and did not take milk well.

There were stretches of months when I was a young child when my grandmother and aunts stayed with us. Mamá Parito, Tía Ana, Tía Maria; names invoked so often and with such familiar affection. Ma'ito, Ti'ana, Ti'mari. Enjambment made them words unto themselves.

Stayed is the wrong word for it. It was not a visit; they came to help my mother. To wash the sheets and cook the afternoon soup, to dress my brother and me in the morning for school and simply be with us, tell us stories, keep us entertained in the hours afterwards when our parents were still at work. I used to understand this reality as being necessary because things like daycare and afterschool programs were well outside the kind of life my parents could afford, which was true. But I've since learned the value of another aspect of it, something richer: that there were people in our lives who had no compunction about dropping everything for months at a time to shepherd my parents through a near-impossible period of parenting two small children under the age of five. There was wealth in this that has continued to pay dividends even now, years after I lost the cadence of the names I called them by.

There were days when the bus dropped us off and I'd sprint the short distance back home, breathing in and out as fast as I could in order to arrive at our door red-faced and raspy, just the kind of out of sorts to ask for my té, a mix of hot honey and ginger and lime that Parito usually made when someone was sick.

"No te haces eso," she told me after one homebound sprint from the bus. She said she'd make me the ginger-lime drink anyway, sick or not. An act of care doesn't need to be earned, she tried to teach me, and simply wanting something can be a need in and of itself.

I USED TO LOVE running. I loved landscapes slowly tumbling past in my peripheral vision; I loved the feeling of a long exhale—the daily rhythms of school seemed to require it. Running downhill to the gravelly scream of the recess bell. Running uphill to the panicky sight of the school bus pulling up at the end of the street. Running phys ed races between portable classrooms that smelled of loam and white glue.

I don't know now if this was for love of the activity so much as being a kid who, simply, could run, and therefore did. That's what happens when you learn to love yourself according to facility. Anyway, it didn't last long: I was ten when I broke my leg, stopped running, and instead started thinking about pain. One summer evening just before school let out, I was playing touch tag on freshly watered grass, running around with the giggly fear of getting caught.

I didn't trip on anything; I simply slipped. I remember hearing a twig snap. For a moment I believed that's what had actually happened. The pain itself wasn't a feeling, but that recess bell ringing somewhere between my ankle and knee. I was so divorced from the sound of my own voice that for a few terrible moments I heard screams that seemed to come from some foreign, animal place without realizing they were coming from my own throat. Alien, untranslatable, even to myself. I can hear, almost thirty years later, the soft door-hinge groan my entire shin bone made before giving in to the weight—a neat little *click*—of its own pressure. When I think about these sounds enough I feel nauseous, even today.

I can tell you what it sounds like to break your tibia clean in two, but I'm not so sure I can tell you what it feels like.

In my experience what's memorable about physical pain isn't so much the sensation itself but the details that stand at the margins, details often easier to communicate. The ability to communicate does not necessarily mean the ability to measure or compare—and more often than not that's precisely the way the world prefers we talk about a universal experience whose individual impacts are anything but.

When Eula Biss thinks about the pain scale in a *Harper's* essay titled after the same, she questions not only contemporary medicine's obsession with finding a method to objectively measure pain, but our collective impulse to drape the feeling over a single hierarchical slope.

"Assigning a value to my own pain has never ceased to feel like a political act," she writes. "People suffer, I know, so that I may eat bananas in February. And then there is history . . ."

The ellipsis is hers. In part, I think, because she realizes that one person or people's pain isn't for someone else to explain.

But to understand? In the pursuit of empathy, this must surely be a goal, even when we know it's impossible. Or perhaps what I mean more specifically is to believe.

My brother used to ham it up for photos. He'd crumple his nose, stick out his tongue, or open his mouth into a fake yawn every time someone forced a snapshot on him. My favourite: a closeup of precisely this kind of face, screaming gape-mouthed at the camera, showing off tiny five-year-old buds of teeth and hands pulling at his head of thick black curls. These days, as a man in his thirties with a scar above his left eye and a purple well in the hollow of his throat where the breathing tube used to be, he refuses to take pictures because he isn't quite as comfortable in his own skin.

He was found bleeding at the foot of a wall once. I visited the site three times afterwards, to see if the tendrils of blood snaking out from where he'd fallen had yet been washed away. The first time, the evidence was still vibrant and thin. The second, flies had taken to sticking themselves in the coagulated slicks. By the third visit, the stains had blackened and retreated into themselves, shrunken proof of when an early morning dog walker had found my brother stumbling in a lake of his own blood, trying to get his phone to work. The man removed his backpack, got him to lie down and rest his head on it, and called an ambulance.

For nearly a month he lay unconscious in an ICU, at first in an induced coma, then intubated, the right side of his skull cracked from the orbital bone upwards. His eye grew and grew to fill the space. He became unrecognizable, a stranger, bandages around an unknown shape. My parents made grieving sounds I'd never before heard in my life. Soft high-pitched wails that came without warning, punctuating their efforts to carry on with life between hospital vigils.

I took the belongings the social worker gave me upon arrival at the hospital, a clear zip-tied garbage bag of blood-soaked jeans and perfectly folded kitchen scrubs and a plastic tub of pad thai tucked into his backpack, the peanuts still evenly sprinkled overtop. The police insisted he had unsuccessfully tried to climb a fence on his way home from work the night before. It partly made sense: hopping a fence and crossing the train tracks on the other side would have cut his walk home in half. It also did not: what kind of fall from a six-foot fence could have done this? My mother kept asking, *Why weren't the peanuts shaken up? How were they still so perfect?*

I kept returning to the site of his injury because I thought concrete answers about what had happened could somehow help. I asked employees at the neighbouring grocery store for security tapes of that night, the concierge at the condo next door about anything he might have heard or seen. No possible answer would have eased my brother's pneumonia, reduced the swelling in his brain, closed up the stoma in his throat. I told myself I was trying to be helpful. In truth I was trying to calm myself, and it was not working.

It's hard to let go of what I used to take as evidence of extreme frailty—pain that transforms the body itself into the punishment rather than something inflicted. There were times under sedation that he still writhed in pain. I watched him slowly rock his head in bandages, from side to side, breathe differently under different medications. What my brother remembers is recovery; everything that happened after his eyes opened and it was clear that he would live.

I cannot forget the sallow colour of the meal replacement shakes he was fed in hospital, and how his knuckles turned the same yellow every time he was force-fed that thick nutritional liquid through a tube in the nose. The wrinkled blue of his hospital gown. How the gown grew big, bigger, too big for him, as the swelling and fluids and painkillers left his body skinny, weak, and quaking, with elbows working double time as he hunched over the aluminum rails of a walker, relearning how to put one foot in front of the other.

Despite this, I don't know what his pain felt like. I don't know what it feels like to fracture your skull in four places, to not know how it happened, to walk home from work one night and wake up one morning weeks later with both of your eyes sealed shut with medical tape. He tried so hard to speak when he couldn't, to walk when he was not yet ready. Some nights the nurses strapped him down to keep him from trying; for a few horrible days a delirium took over, convincing him there was poison in the feeding bags. He became a stranger to himself, then, too—his own type of howl. He told me this often. I wouldn't know how to escape that proof of one's own frailty. I didn't immediately understand why someone might try.

Despite the coma, the cracked skull, the fact that he has permanently lost sight in his right eye, my brother speaks of this experience the way one might of a religious apparition, when he speaks of it at all.

Some senses, he says, are heightened. He will smell a note of coffee in the burning cigarette of someone passing him on the street. Other times, changes manifest themselves in ways that are unpredictable and, once in a while, seemingly a complete betrayal of the person he was before the fall. He used to live for the movies; he's barely set foot in a theatre in the ten years since. He rarely argues about anything political anymore, his "who cares?" shrug communicating something closer to "who am I to say?"

One thing has remained the same, if not intensified: he works. Too much, I thought back then, and often still do. Six weeks after he woke up, he was back in the kitchen. He'd pull double shifts as a manager at a steak house, crouching in front of ovens and hunching over cast iron pans in tiny, oppressively hot spaces, as he had done for years—for ten hours straight, more on weekends. He insisted on it. "It's good for me," he'd repeat, and it took a while for me to believe this.

DAD, ARE YOU TAKING me to Rhea's? I told her I'd be there like thirty minutes ago.

One second, bunch. Why am I taking you there again?

School project.

About what?

Uh . . . history?

Whose history?

Something about the conquistadors.

Oh, bunch! Why didn't you tell me? You know I have all the books. Is it about La China Poblana?

Uh, no? You do know you can't call people chinas, right?

Why?

Because it's racist, Dad.

China means "Oriental" in this context, bunch. And people from India, or anywhere in the East, were called chinas back then. It's like saying "an Oriental."

That's still racist! You can't say "Oriental"! What does the East even mean?

What's racist about the word *Oriental*? It's a generalized word.

That's not the same thing! This is stupid. Can we stop?

I just want you to explain to me how the word *Oriental* is racist. Is this some PC thing?

I really don't want to talk about this anymore. I'm going to be late. Can we go?

WHEN I WAS THE age you are now, older than seven and younger than a teen, I had this ritual for how I'd get ready for a family trip to Vallarta. Your pa would book the plane tickets, always by phone, and often on speaker so that we could all sit in the kitchen and listen to the flight details.

There was a bit of ceremony to it, and a bit of wish fulfillment, too: he would sometimes call up a hotline that listed last-minute flight deals to warm cities across the continent. *Holguín, six days seven nights. San José, five days four nights.* He'd window-shop this way for a little while until my mother hung up the phone.

When the flight was confirmed I'd write the times out in an empty workbook, along with a list of the things I needed to wear, and an agenda for what I imagined I'd do— though I rarely made it past the second day on that count. Sometimes I packed nail polishes ahead of time, because I so badly wanted to know what my time there would be like.

This is how I will meet my cousins, the book I will read on the plane. This is the nail colour I will wear on the beach.

My fear then, as it sometimes is now, wasn't that we'd miss our plane, or that it would run out of fuel mid-flight and fall into the sea. I wasn't afraid I'd throw up during takeoff or end up lost to my family forever during some layover. I was worried that, should any of those things happen, I wouldn't know what to do.

Always knowing what will happen isn't possible, and to try is a fool's pursuit. I have often instead relied on the belief that it is always possible to know *what* to do in any given circumstance—for the longest time not realizing that this is simply another version of the same problem. Search engines, menstrual apps, product reviews: so many facets of how we live today permit, and even encourage, a certain kind of thinking. *There is always a right answer. It is always possible to know what to do.* The work of the anxious is to unlearn this lesson, over and over.

And sometimes it truly is work. The weeks after your uncle's accident were a hazy, low-frequency hum of rotating statements from doctors—sometimes contradictory—about whether he would live or die, see again, walk again, speak. The day the nurse told us he would be ready to come off intubation soon was the first time I left the house to see friends. That evening your Mamá Rú called me with an update; he had developed pneumonia, she'd been told, and might not last the night. "Your brother is very sick," she said on the phone, in a measured way that frightened me. On and on it went like this, for weeks. No level of attention to his sedative dosage or vitals could change the outcome; nothing could be *done*.

And sometimes, it is not work. It can be an event, inevitable. A month after he was admitted, I walked into your uncle's hospital room to find him looking at me. Truly *looking* and able to see me, even with one eye shut. He greeted me with a gesture I will keep with me for the rest of my life: his first three digits extended, pinky and ring finger slightly curled. A wave as he has always done, truly the essence of him, even when hindered by the weighted blanket of tubes and a post-propofol haze. *Hi*. Joy can settle over you; its arrival is the announcement. I didn't need to know anything else.

ONE TIME, I DIDN'T prepare. Shortly before David Bowie died and Prince died and everyone acted as though this was proof positive the world was going to end (for people inclined to think this way, it was going to—just not yet), I didn't pack, almost forgot my passport, barely made it in time to meet your grandmother at the airport to fly to Vallarta.

At the gate we encountered a woman travelling alone with three children. Two—a boy and a girl slightly younger than you are now—were playing tag in and around the seats, while a third, younger, sat in a tiny collapsible lawn chair next to two carry-on suitcases, watching bubbly, high-pitched cartoons on an iPad.

A flight attendant announced that it was time to board, and the woman corralled her children. She instructed the two older ones to stand by one of the suitcases while she pulled the other one close to herself and removed two nylon straps from its front pocket. Without removing the youngest child from the chair, she tied its backrest to the front of the suitcase with the first strap going over his belly. She then looped the second one underneath the seat and over the top handle of the case, gently tightened both belts, and rolled off with all three of her children.

I don't know if it was the impromptu suitcase-stroller, or the masterful way she at once pretended not to speak English and smirked as the flight attendant admonished her for the makeshift contraption, for apparently putting her child in danger, for her multiple suitcases, for all but travelling alone with three children, for the *too much* of her. But something about this scene made me picture my grandmother, flying home to Vallarta with me while my mother convalesced from a difficult pregnancy. My mother, flying alone at twenty-six with two screaming, farting toddlers in tow. Myself one day, in transit with a child. In transit to anywhere; the destination didn't matter. I knew I wanted this. I hadn't yet started thinking about acting upon this desired future, much less discussed it with your dad.

I didn't know that I didn't have to. I was already pregnant when watching that mother; pregnant when I got on the plane with a headache like a closing vice; pregnant when I greeted my family and sat down to asada; pregnant when I fell asleep on the red comforter of my grandmother's bed, her reciting the rosary in the same room, the ceiling fan whirring overhead.

IT'S DISORIENTING AND FRIGHTENING to realize how hard you can come to love something without thinking for too long about its existence. Here is one way to fall in love with an idea.

First, feel a twinge in your abdomen and left breast while watching a terrible horror movie, and despite having never felt the need to, pull out a pregnancy test because you're horrified by a new and distinct awareness of what's happening in your own skin. When the test comes up positive, cry on the couch for an hour until your husband comes home, and take four more tests that he picks up at your request just to be sure. Go to a doctor for yet another test. Start taking vitamins.

Call your mother, who immediately starts crocheting white cotton receiving blankets and makes plans to retire early. Freak out about the interminable graduate degree you've been working on. Scour the city for prenatal yoga classes that don't cost you the firstborn you're taking the classes for in the first place. Sign up for email newsletters that mark the growth of your baby in food metaphors, despite having despised the cartoonification of prescribed women's narratives all your life.

Find yourself pulling a complete one-eighty after getting fish-hooked on the beachy smell of vinegary ketchup and food-court French fries during lunch hour, and giggle. Allow your husband to talk to your stomach each night: *goodnight lentil, goodnight blueberry, goodnight jellybean*. Feel ashamed of this for a minute, and then angry with yourself that you felt ashamed in the first place.

Search frantically for a midwife in a province where demand has far outstripped availability, and get placed on every waitlist in the city while hoping an obstetrician can see you in at least the first eight weeks. Spend New Year's passing off glasses of club soda as gin and tonic. Open up a savings account to squirrel away dollars for an education fund. You're just barely two months pregnant. You've told no one beyond your parents, and one or two friends who are parents themselves.

One of these friends gifts you the loveliest hand-me-down: a pale yellow onesie with the words *Fuck The Patriarchy* silkscreened in faded purple cursive across the chest. Some nights, you allow yourself to unfold that little piece of clothing, and imagine a tiny, wiggling body filling it out.

For a few weeks after you don't need to do so anymore, you sometimes still do.

There is a very convincing feeling of control that the secrecy of early pregnancy affords you. At a time when you're still trying to plan for parental leave or whether or not that extra cup of coffee is going to brain-damage your would-be child, you have a say over who knows, and when—and therefore whose advice you care to solicit before the relentless firehose stream of instructions from extended family, co-workers, and random people off the street begins.

But to be newly pregnant is also to feel uniquely unsafe. If not from crushing uncertainty over timing, childcare, and ideas about parenthood, then about the pregnancy itself. Commonly cited numbers suggest 10 to 20 per cent of all pregnancies end in miscarriage, about 80 per cent of which happen in the first twelve weeks. What we unquestioningly call common sense suggests this is precisely the reason for the three-month rule of telling. After her own miscarriage, Alexandra Kimball wrote in the *Globe and Mail* about the bind in this logic. "A woman who does not announce her early pregnancy will not have to announce its loss: She can move on in privacy as if it never happened."

The very real danger beyond pregnancy loss itself, she writes, is in the statistical likelihood of having to do precisely this. Move on as though it never happened.

While at an out-of-town conference for work, for example, I might have chosen to tell the concierge at the hotel I was staying at why I needed a taxi just ten minutes after I'd checked in, and immediately. After kicking my shoes off in the freshly turned-over room, two cramps shot from my navel downwards, violent arrows of pain that came and went at their leisure. I could have told the taxi driver to speed up because I was worried I was having a miscarriage, but to use the actual words felt too final. Even in triage I could only describe symptoms. Even while it was happening, I couldn't announce it.

Instead, I shuffled from waiting room to waiting room in a hospital shift and black high heels, the only shoes I'd brought with me on the trip. I zeroed in on irrelevant details for distraction. The Salvadorean Spanish my neighbour in the ER used to describe his unbearable headache. The pink and navy lettering on the sweatshirt of a young woman crying inconsolably. While my husband was rushing to this hospital two hours away at likely illegal speeds, I was making hopeful, just-in-case arrangements to head back to the conference I hadn't yet shown up for.

I remember wincing because I hadn't shaved my legs beforehand, and smiling at the curly-haired nurses who took my blood, handed me cups of water with ice chips, and rubbed ultrasound gel on my belly with the pragmatic cheer of seasoned frontline healthcare workers who truly love their work. *How's the cramping, honey? Is the water too cold?* Until they were armed with the paperwork to tell me so, they never used the word, either.

Forty minutes before my husband arrived, a nurse-practitioner with plastic-framed glasses perched at the tip of her nose used that paperwork, rolled up, to open the curtains of the last waiting room. "Okay," she said with a little too much breath. "Here's why we think you're having a miscarriage." My hCG hormone levels were too low. The cramping was too frequent to be the round ligament pain that's otherwise relatively normal for early-stage pregnancy. I hadn't yet had an ultrasound, and this first one was being delivered only as a written report. Gestational sac identified. Fetal pole identified. No fetal heart rate demonstrated during the exam.

I worried over that last detail in my head like a little set of prayer beads for the twenty minutes before my husband arrived, while the nurse went out to get painkillers, and those painful arrows opened up into a pitilessly violent bleed that sent me shivering into a single-unit bathroom.

"It's okay," another nurse told me a couple of hours later, while handing me a little cup of Tylenol 3s and a pack of hospital-grade menstrual pads. "I see this happen to so many women, every month." She rattled off my statistical chances of successfully making a child. "Talk with your doctor first, but you can usually try this again in as little as eight weeks."

On my most insomniac nights as a child, I'd resort to one last step before waking up my parents in tears about being unable to sleep: counting the lit windows, looking past my backyard to the condo buildings nearby to bulk up the number of people who were still awake with me in those late-night hours. To transpose this habit to my circumstances today, imagine 37,000 windows lit for having lost a pregnancy. That's how many parents in my province alone experience this type of loss each year, from miscarriage to stillbirth.

Despite this, the idea of what mourning should look like after losing a wanted pregnancy remains troubled in contemporary culture. Fiction and pop culture are rife with it as an occurrence, but it is more often than not employed as a plot device, a fulcrum on which to pivot some larger, seemingly more important narrative.

Before I left the hospital, a final nurse handed me a doctor's note recommending a couple of days off work and a printed-out list of things to expect over the next six weeks. I might continue to bleed. I shouldn't use tampons.

I should avoid medications not approved by my doctor and head back to an ER if I developed a fever or chills.

Here are a couple of things that the fact sheet and my family doctor at the time didn't warn me about upfront: I bled in an infuriating stop-start pattern for six weeks. Angry constellations of acne flared up along my back and jawline. In some regards my body still thought it was pregnant; it kept growing, and hurt in bone joints everywhere, all the time. The fatigue I'd felt beforehand atomized from a desire to sleep to an overwhelming need to move as little as possible. I picked fights with my husband. I planned as many social events as I could with friends who didn't know, in an attempt to feel normal. Not twenty-four hours after coming home from the hospital, I kept brunch plans with friends in an absurdly pristine Paris-themed café, loaded up with layers of sterile cotton and codeine.

This, in retrospect, was perhaps the most alarming thing: that I thought I could feel normal, and so soon after.

The truth is, in this overall experience I was relatively very lucky. I have since read stories of women who go hours after first noticing symptoms—sometimes days—before receiving the examinations that can confirm their fears. Of others who have had to have follow-up dilation and curettage procedures performed in the hospital's maternity unit, among new parents. In some cases, a fetus is removed and left in the room with the parents. Often, at least where I live, a doctor doesn't refer patients to the kinds of perinatal programs that specifically deal with miscarriage aftercare, and which seek to identify causes, until they've lost a pregnancy three times.

The first week I knew I was pregnant, I went to buy a maternity bra. It was early days, but already much of what I owned was pinching, stretching, and imprinting seams into my skin.

"How far along are you?" the sales associate asked, adjusting the straps and pulling at the tarp-like material. "You don't look that uncomfortable." Of course, I very much was.

"Eight weeks," I said. I was three.

It was the first time I'd tried to justify pain, as if pain ever needed such a thing, and it continued for weeks after the miscarriage, along with a few other changes. Tension liked to rest in my right jaw, so I'd crack it the way some crack their knuckles. I shaved my legs more often in preparation for emergencies that might or might not materialize. I became a far more indecisive person, and agonized over seemingly insignificant choices. Shortly after I bought that bra, I stuffed it in a drawer to wait and see if my discomfort would eventually become as evident to others as it felt to me.

Only in the weeks after I stopped preparing for a different outcome did I allow myself to take it out, still wrapped in its flaxen tissue, and think about the future. It felt as though choosing to keep it or get rid of it might signal some kind of decision about whether or not to try again. But I did not decide, and I kept it regardless.

DAD, DID YOU HAVE a moustache when I was born?

No, why?

There's just this baby picture I remember of you holding me up in a yellow hat. You had a moustache in it.

Oh, no bunch. That was your brother. He was wearing your hat.

Oh.

He wore a lot of your things, as a baby. He even slept in your crib, the one Uncle gave you, with a lamb on it.

I had a dream about him the other night. Uncle.

Oh?

Yeah. It was weird, because even in the dream I knew he was gone? And so did he? It was as though it was taking place in some afterlife. He had a party in this big mansion on the shore of a beach. You were there. Everyone was there. I remember finding a massive closet filled with empty cans of tomato sauce. And he couldn't sit in chairs because of the thing in his hips.

That's . . . a beautiful dream, bunch.

Yeah, he told me he was going to be okay. But anyway, we should go to St. Mike's now. Visiting hours are almost over.

WHEN I WAS EIGHT, your pa took my brother and me to Chapultepec, a castle that sits atop a volcanic rock hill from which most of Mexico City can be seen. Over the past half-millennium this hill has had many lives. As a sacred space for the Nahua people who made a home there; a summer palace for the Spanish viceroys whose military forcibly took this land from them; a training academy for the then-Mexican military fighting off American forces; the palace of a French-appointed emperor whose short-lived reign followed the Mexican-American War; a presidential residence; a national history museum; and, in the year I was born, a UNESCO World Heritage Site. Many places of cascading empire are put out to pasture this way.

At the castle's domed entrance, Pa instructed us to look up. A mural painted across the dome showed a young man, possibly a teenager, falling through the ceiling, through the air, wrapped in a flag and weeping. Painted in the late 1960s to memorialize the events of the 1847 Battle of

Chapultepec, a landmark event in the Mexican–American War, it honoured six teenage cadets who refused to retreat from battle. One, Juan Escutia, wrapped himself in the castle's flag and flung himself from its towers, ensuring that neither he nor the symbolic piece of cloth would be taken by American soldiers.

In that era of the hill's life, Chapultepec Castle was a military academy housing children as young as ten. The youngest of Los Niños Héroes, as they are known now, was thirteen. Five of the six were born into military families; by the time they'd been sent off for training, their parents had lived through a decade of war with Spain and another of extreme political instability. It's hard to believe they didn't know the nature of their children's future.

An eight-year-old is prone to literal thinking. When my father told us this story, pointing to the mural's tendrils of smoke, violent lines, and wound-like colours, I remember genuinely believing such a sacrifice might still be expected of a young adult today—celebrated, even. I remember knowing for certain I didn't have it in me. Most cities in Mexico have at least one street that bears the name Los Niños.

We walked out to the black-and-white-tiled veranda that wraps around much of the castle's exterior. I poked my head through the stone railing, over the edge of the hill, and looked down upon the rocks that cascaded to the bottom. I wanted to know how long that boy fell for.

IN 1966, OR PERHAPS 1965, two American writers vacation somewhere in Mexico. At some point along the trip, they gaze at a map of the country. They are taken by the eastern slice of a peninsula that reaches out into the many-blued waters where the Gulf of Mexico and the Caribbean Sea meet—its name enticing, mysterious. "The place on the map called Quintana Roo was still frequented mainly by archaeologists, herpetologists, and bandits," Joan Didion writes in *Blue Nights*. "The institution that became spring break in Cancún did not yet exist. There were no bargain flights. There was no Club Med. The place on the map called Quintana Roo was still terra incognita." The perfect condition, the perfect name, she reasons a few months later, for her newly adopted daughter, whom she also describes as such: *terra incognita*.

People I knew loved to spell out the fact of this name after vacationing in the area—sometimes in a story or anecdote, sometimes in an Instagram post, this knowledge almost always made possible by the very machinations of tourism whose absence, for Didion, imbued the place with mystery and the potential for a different type of personal claim. *She named her daughter after it!*

For years, this detail annoyed me more than it should have. A name on a map is not some opportunity to build a personal myth, I'd think to myself. The name and the fact of the map itself—the logic behind its necessity, the series of acts that led to its creation—already represent a version of that. As Lee Maracle wrote: "Maps are always old."

Perhaps also because Didion's writing about it suggested an almost incurious regard that seemed out of step with what I otherwise loved about her writing. It annoyed me that such things as bargain flights and spring break would be considered necessary in order to render a place like this—or any place—knowable. I was annoyed, perhaps, at being reminded in a quick succession of quotes, small fragments, of how much my enjoyment of her work required a consistent low-dose suspension of disbelief.

Didion and her husband, John Dunne, brought their daughter home after a final California courthouse adoption hearing. "*L'adoptada,* she came to be called in the household. The adopted one," she writes. Later, when Didion and Dunne took Quintana to a restaurant after the adoption was finalized: "*Qué hermosa,* the waiters crooned. *Qué chula.*"

The insertion of another language and, by extension, an elision of everything else—the fact of the servers, housekeepers, childcare, a structure-making constant presence that made their lives as they were possible. When one's life is structured this way, why wouldn't a map produce a name without history, without complication?

A couple of years ago, Myriam Gurba articulated this problem in a way likely most recognizable to West Coast Mexican Americans who grew up reading Didion's name conflated with the idea of California. "[Didion] modeled how writing yourself into the story of a place convinces readers that the place is yours . . . Your body joins the topography," Gurba wrote, in an essay for the website Electric Literature, at once praising the brisk intelligence of Didion's work and excoriating what she identified as its racial grammar, a term coined by sociologist Eduardo Bonilla-Silva to describe rules that govern how a society underpinned by a white supremacist structure understands race and the way we talk about it.

I hold much of Didion's work close to me. I can read her work and touch her grief. But there isn't a single written spotlight on a place that hasn't had to be split into its constituent colours—the truths selected, unselected, not known. "The place on the map called Quintana Roo was still yet not a state but a territory," she writes, to emphasize its lack of legitimacy; it was less known, less real. In truth, years of resistance to being subsumed by the Mexican state—part Mayan, part not—was the underlying reason for its territory status. The wave of travel that Didion and Dunne represented preceded the land's eventual incorporation into statehood in 1974.

Andrés Quintana Roo, one of the co-creators of the Mexican Declaration of Independence, was someone before this place, before the daughter of a writer. Before his name became that place in 1902, the land was home to Chan Santa Cruz, an independent Maya nation that fought the state for its sovereignty for almost seventy years. Before that, Ekab and Uaymil. Before that, the cradle of where a rock the size of a small country rammed into the Earth, ending non-avian dinosaur life. A place upon another upon another, folded over itself many times over.

This is true of Quintana Roo. It's true of Didion's California too, whose suburbs D.J. Waldie saw straight through: "Before they put a grid over it, and restrained the ground from indifference, any place was as good as any other."

I USED TO THINK I hated tourists. I used to think I knew what one was.

Definitions facilitate distance. This, in turn, can allow one the luxury of judgement. A person can know these two things and still fail to avoid leaning too heavily on both in their own life. I built my definition of tourists on widely accepted images of the wrong way to travel. The Hawaiian-print button-down shirt and oversized camera strap. Fanny packs full of maps. Loud, obnoxious comments in airport security lines about how slowly things move in *this* part of the world. Reflexive distrust of taxi drivers, beach vendors, servers—anyone in a position to accept the money a tourist had come there to spend. Limp iceberg salads in all-inclusive resort buffets. Sunburns. Litter. The ridiculous notion that novelty drinking vessels, regardless of their content, are somehow indicative of the local culture's proclivity for fun. The glasses can show up anywhere—Vallarta, Varadero, Cayo Coco, Cancún—and must, for they are one of the things that sand down the contours and details of each of these places into the same experience.

And later: the pernicious insistence on an authentic experience. *Show me your world before all of this. Before the hotels, the tour buses, the teetering neighbourhoods built quickly to house the people who came to cook the food and change the sheets and mind the door at the nightclubs and rake our trash from the sand in the morning. Who were you before then?*

It felt good to hold contempt for this type of tourism, and therefore this type of person. It and they were bad for the world. In most respects, this still holds true. There is travel that fosters no real understanding or empathy for the places you go to and the people you meet there; that consumes irresponsible amounts of water, energy, and resources for the benefit of hospitality conglomerates that are rarely locally owned.

The first time I read Jamaica Kincaid, I thought I identified with her contempt. "The thing you have always suspected about yourself the minute you become a tourist is true," she writes in *A Small Place*. "A tourist is an ugly human being." I knew she meant the kind of person who might treat another part of the world as an uncomplicated paradise, untroubled by history. The kind of person who benefits from most of history's uglier plotlines.

"You make a leap from being that nice blob just sitting like a boob in your amniotic sac of the modern experience to being a person visiting heaps of death and ruin and feeling alive and inspired at the sight of it; to being a person lying on some faraway beach, your stilled body stinking and glistening in the sand." Tourists, turds, melting in the heat. Caribbean or Pacific; it is still the same sun that shines on any place as good as any other.

DURING A BRIEF TIME in food service at a national chain restaurant, I learned early on to identify the type of diner especially flattered by any acknowledgement of expertise, regardless of whether such expertise wasn't so much knowledge as opinion, or even accurate. Such diners want to be seen not as customers but as conspirators, excited by the idea of demonstrating for exhausted women in black skirts and uniform-issue high heels the long *a* in the pronunciation of *naan* with their watery butter chicken, or that they too are keenly aware that pad thai should not be made with ketchup.

For a while, I didn't mind this kind of interaction. Tables such as these were predictable and easy to please— and, being barely out of my teens, I often mistook this quality for kindness. These diners were different than the high-strung people given to asking for the manager over a bent straw in a glass of soda, or who were convinced I'd added an item to their bill without asking. A woman once stopped her daughter from thanking me for placing her apple and Brie grilled cheese sandwich on the table, because, as she explained to her, people shouldn't be thanked for doing their job. After that interaction, I couldn't unsee it: the porous veil people actively cast over those engaged in any type of service work, filtering out their personhood, capable at any point of negating them completely should whatever desired act of service or care not be performed to their liking.

One night, I was assigned to the table of a couple who were returning at the restaurant's invitation. They had been so unimpressed by their previous experience that they'd written to the general manager to express their dissatisfaction at what they'd been served. It was the beginning of my shift. One of them looked me over twice before giving his instructions.

"I want a *real* margarita. Do you know how that's made?"

Imagine: a pink, freckled man in a polo shirt with a nicotine-yellowed beard looking a twenty-year-old dead in the eye and asking a question like this. At this particular restaurant we were: not allowed to wear flat shoes; not allowed to wear opaque tights; all but required to flirt with patrons in the lounge section of the dining room, in which men were not allowed to wait tables. But no interaction I'd had in such an environment, tableside or otherwise, embarrassed me as much as this one. Perhaps in part because of how I participated in it, too: I picked up their drink menus, cardboard slates covered in PVC pressed to look like leather, and did my best to smile.

"You know, most customers come in here expecting some sugary slushies with tequila when they ask for those," I said. "But you mean *en rocas*, right?" I rolled my *r*'s better than in any Saturday Spanish-school diction test. This was good. It was, in fact, more than enough.

"The social equivalent of playing dead is to put forward a façade," Nuar Alsadir writes in *Animal Joy*. While she is talking about pediatrician and psychoanalyst Donald Winnicott's theories on a person's ability to express themselves completely free of socialized codes, the idea of performing authenticity as a version of playing dead—a self-negating cousin to code-switching—is a sickeningly accurate description of more of my earlier memories than I'd like to admit, whether or not it was for my own benefit.

It has been almost twenty years, but I remember the chit very clearly. Two glasses of an Ontario sauvignon blanc. A green curry chicken on rice, provenance unspecified. Steak frites, a house special. Two of those "authentic" unblended margaritas, made with gasoline tequila and served in glasses shoved directly into rock salt, instead of rolled at a slight angle to avoid over-seasoning the drink. It was the best tip I ever received at that job. It was also the most instructive.

THE AUTUMN AFTER YOUR brother was born, when you were four years old, I left a screening of Pedro Almodóvar's *Parallel Mothers* with Emily. Its final scene is an extended shot that pans the length of an exhumed mass grave of victims of the Francoist regime, nearly identical to those the Spanish government had recently, in real life, federally voted to excavate. In both plot and reality, the point is to return the taken and murdered to the living—to relatives who can still recall their names and faces.

Almodóvar has been making movies about two things for much of his career: mothers, and Spain's lingering reluctance to come to terms with its post-fascism hangover. Emily said as much afterwards, while we snacked on plates of warmed olives and little fried fishes at a café down the street from the theatre. But when she said it, she clarified the pattern: "He has been making a version of this movie his whole life." This wasn't a knock. She meant it as reverence. Transcendent art often comes from repetition, turning one idea over and over many times in your mind, returning to it, examining each facet and cut. Its retelling is what makes the story whole, legible, real.

For Almodóvar, these two themes are first demonstrated though rejection. *Labyrinth of Passion*, *What Have I Done to Deserve This?*, and his other early Movida Madrileña films revel in precisely the aspects of life the Francoist regime sought to suppress. Hedonistic, anarchic, sexually liberated colour onscreen. And then: cradles, graves, and ghosts. In *Live Flesh*, a baby is born at the dawn of Spain's transition to democracy. In *Volver*, a mother returns from the dead to correct the agonies inflicted upon her daughter in childhood.

But *Mothers*, and its final scene in particular, is the story distilled to a drop. *Look at the bodies*, he tells you. Look at them: the bones of the father holding his child's plastic rattle; a grandfather's storied glass eye. See the mourners who have insisted on their right to look upon and carry the remains home. Granddaughters, great-granddaughters, mostly women and many of them mothers who remember what their loved ones were wearing the night of their abduction. Two of these mothers were also lovers once. One daughter died of SIDS in the cradle; the other, now a toddler, is also looking upon the graves. One mother learns before the other that their daughters were switched at birth. *Es una película Almodóvar, ¿entiendes?*

The year we watched *Mothers*, teams of archaeologists and volunteers were also looking for graves not too far from where we lived. They conducted interviews with survivors and descendants of Indigenous children the Canadian state had taken away from their families to attend cultural genocide factories disguised as assimilation camps disguised as schools; many of them did not return. The children in these institutions were abused, poorly fed to the point of malnutrition, experimented on, left susceptible to breakouts of fatal disease, and violently and cruelly cut off from their own origins: family, language, culture, home. The research teams used ground-penetrating radar, a kind of earth ultrasound, which was rolled over portions of land again and again like a lawnmower.

That spring, Tk'emlúps te Secwépemc announced finding physical evidence of a mass grave of upwards of 215 children near Kamloops Indian Residential School in southeastern British Columbia. By the end of the year, another five communities would make similar announcements: Cowessess First Nation, Lower Kootenay Band, Penelakut Tribe, Sioux Valley Dakota Nation, and ʔaq̓am First Nation. There have been many more since.

This wasn't the first time this type of story had been told about Canada's residential school system. Investigations into unmarked grave sites date back to the mid-1970s;

the stories of survivors go back decades further. But the horrifying announcement was, seemingly, the first to force the world to take notice. To news outlets across the globe: *we know where their bodies are.* And to those for whom Canada is a chosen inheritance, which includes you and me: this was done in the name of your ability to tell an origin story of your own on this land, even if that story has its own pain. Tend to your origins, yes, but do not let how you speak about them be used as a distraction. Do not look away.

I WENT TO SEE a movie alone at the Carlton Cinema in the last few weeks before you were born. Though I haven't in years, I love to go to the theatre on my own, and the Carlton is one of my favourites. Each room is so tiny, the theatres are too small for aisles. Its maroon carpets, compact screens, sticky floors, the illicit rustle of bagged candy from the bulk shop next door: it's the feeling of watching a movie in someone's rec room with a dozen strangers. Despite the necessity of climbing stairs to reach its entrance, it has the feel of a basement. When I lived down the street as an undergrad student, I'd spend $2 on a bag of gummies and $4 on a matinee ticket. The best thrill, conveniently cheap, and one I indulged in religiously for years.

It was November, the greyest part of the year, and Donald Trump had just been elected president of the United States. In the newsroom where I worked at the time, colleagues had just lost bets over the results and were recalibrating their sense of the world order, despite only a few years earlier having seen a similarly yellow-haired buffoon take office in Toronto and proceed to subject the city to extreme civic mismanagement and global humiliation.

I eased myself into a front-row seat with a quarter-pound of Swedish Berries and stared up at the screen, eight and a half months pregnant. I was achy, happy, and ready to cry at any kind of movie that popped up on the screen. I didn't know a child would die within the first ten minutes of the film.

Arrival is intended to be a film about language. Adapted from Ted Chiang's "Story of Your Life," it features grand, sweeping scenes of misty grasslands in locations all over the world that have been visited by massive alien spacecraft, each the elegant ovoid shape of a well-filed nail. These ships are staffed by teams of squid-like aliens responsible for teaching humankind their language in order to communicate the reason for their appearance. Only one group of human researchers is successful in learning it—the Americans. Amy Adams plays Louise, a quietly determined linguist who connects with the beings and, by virtue of learning their language and writing system, changes the way she experiences time. By the end of the film she is able to see what has been, is happening, and will be, all at once. It is suggested this knowledge has implications both universal and personal. The audience watches Adams talk a military official down from a set of actions that may start a global conflict, and, minutes later, accept a future in which she becomes the mother of a child who will die before she turns fifteen.

It isn't clear to the viewer in that moment, but in watching the opening sequence they know how the movie ends, before it really gets started. The revelation itself isn't so much the film's structure, but the truth we were meant to understand all along: a woman chooses to become a mother despite knowing she will outlive her child. At the time, and as pregnant as I was, I burst into tears. I left my last few Swedish Berries at the concessions counter and waddled out of the building.

When I was five, your grandmother took me to an audiologist for a hearing test. I remember sitting in a dark, soundproofed booth with a pair of headphones on; looking out at the adults through a small plastic window; holding a little joystick with a red button I was instructed to press any time I heard a beeping sound. I remember listening hard, wanting to excel at this exercise that had absolutely zero stakes. I knew my hearing was fine.

I didn't learn until years later that my kindergarten teacher had requested I take this test. I don't remember being asked multiple times if I understood English, or to stop speaking Spanish to the other kids in class, or any of the teacher's other instructions I apparently didn't follow, which had led her to think I had a hearing problem. I do know that I was used to speaking how I wanted, something that shrank away over time as my Spanish deteriorated.

I don't see those two things as causally related, exactly, but before I watched you acquire language of your own I'd often wonder about that version of me—someone who shared a first way of speaking with her mother. Singing the lullabies to me that she grew up with; saying *pórtense bien* instead of *goodbye*. For a long time, I'd have a visceral reaction to hearing those words. They'd open up something in me that felt like sitting in that soundproof pod, as though the window was much smaller than I'd originally thought, as though much of my childhood was and still is sitting somewhere in my brain unremembered. Even the touchable fragments have the quality of a dream.

Children learn to identify objects as singular things, and then they learn to categorize. This is as much the process of learning to speak as it is the building of a framework for how one understands the world. It is also essential: without categorization, every unfamiliar object or situation would be experienced completely anew—a fact that sounds lovely in theory only to those who've already learned about the world through categorization.

An infant learns to call those who love them by name. Maybe one of these names is Mamá. For the child, this word is for a singular person, and represents a singular relationship. But the person being called Mamá is at the disadvantage of having learned that this word is a category, too. It describes a role, often with prescriptions. Perhaps this knowledge sometimes gets in the way.

When you were new to running and new to wearing sandals, you tried doing both together and tripped on the sidewalk, skinning your knee for the first time. I fanned the little wound to air it out, and put on your first Band-Aid. You learned to say *booboo*, and you didn't cry.

I thought you'd simply learned to say a new word. But within a day, you saw booboos everywhere. The pillow with a ripped seam, the toy missing a piece, the little purple scar in the well of your tio's throat. *Booboo? Booboo?* It wasn't just a word you'd learned; it was a category, and you were seeking out examples. It seemed you could find a wound in everything, but rather than seeing this as a child learning about their environment, I took it to be an indicator of your outlook on a life you'd barely begun, an outlook not all that unlike mine. *Just like Mommy*, I thought. How dim. You've long since stopped talking about wounds, and I am grateful for it; I am still trying to unlearn the inclination.

You taught me language, too. Every grammatically fuzzy turn of phrase and compound word you and your brother made up in your first years of life: asking "what you said?"; calling something untrustworthy or gross "scamey"; asking "what it doin?" as a request for more information about an unfamiliar object. You sometimes still speak this way. I never correct you. I want to remember these phrases long after the world has plucked them from your mouth. I want to save them for you, but I also want them for me.

"When children are very young, you are the director of the play of their life," Rivka Galchen writes. "Later you have front-row seats for what is happening with them. Then maybe fourth-row seats. They get older, and you, the parents, get to watch from the front of the mezzanine. But you keep getting moved farther back. Eventually you're so far, you're in the seats they used to call paradise."

I am starting to see through my mother's eyes how language is one of the ways this movement happens—and that this description is also accurate for how one forgets a way of speaking. There's a saying my mother used to bark out in exasperation when I'd purposely hide from her in department stores as a kid, or when my brother would chew up, then spit out, the peas in his rice: "¡Que coraje me da contigo!" It means "I'm angry with you," but *coraje* can translate to both "irritation" and "courage" in English, so I'd sometimes purposely flip it and pretend my mother was asking for the courage to parent a wandering brat and a relentlessly picky eater.

I used to dwell on how this Spanglish way of interpreting events was once possible. I now know that this mode of speaking made a certain version of parenthood possible for my mother, too. Parents create a language with their children, a way of speaking they are destined to outgrow.

I have a tidy little dialogue I'm quite used to performing when talking about fluency in public. Someone asks me about something or other in Spanish. On the bus, while travelling, at the Apple counter of a Best Buy. I don't know why it's Spanish specifically; I don't think my physical appearance draws a direct line to how I speak, nor do I think there's a specific set of characteristics that could universally suggest such a thing. Given the violent history of this language's trajectory across the globe, how could there be?

"Mi'ijita dice que quiere un iPad. ¿Comprarias esto?"

My daughter says she wants an iPad. Would you buy this for a little girl?

"¿Creo que si? Si sabe que ella lo usaron."

I think so? If I know she used it.

I don't have an accent; I haven't stuttered. But I have the grammar of a toddler and my speech is odd. The man has rectangular bifocals attached to a glasses chain. He takes them off and folds them up to look at me, and I already know what I need to say:

"Perdóname. Entiendo todo perfectamente, pero no

Forgive me. I can understand you perfectly but I don't

habla muy bien. He olvidado mucho."

speak very well—I've forgotten so much.

I've said this phrase so many times, in exactly this way, it's become all I believe about my relationship to this language.

That I say *perdóname* instead of *disculpe*—that I'm more

forgive me   *sorry*

comfortable with asking forgiveness—is just another example of the problem. This person was just shopping for an iPad; asking for directions; trying to sell me bus tickets. Why should they care about my relationship to how I speak?

How is my discomfort and its attendant problems something to forgive?

Once, in my early twenties, this happened at a jewellery store that doubled as a bus stop. I'd taken a trip with two friends to Playacar, a hotel neighbourhood south of Playa del Carmen, which itself is its own small town south of Cancún—a sort of cascade of tourism-driven development. The resort's transportation into the city was free so long as you spent twenty minutes browsing a two-storey building filled with emerald-studded jaguars, opal collars, and Aztec calendars etched into gold and silver flatware. It was immediately clear to anyone working there we weren't buying anything. The sales associate, an exceedingly kind man who looked like Alex Trebek in a three-piece pinstripe suit, didn't try.

Pero quería saber: ¿de dónde estás?

But he wanted to know: where was I from?

Le dije la misma historia. My own personal business card.

I told the same story.

"No te preocupes, cariño. It's in your blood."

"Don't worry, honey. Es la sangre que corre en tus venas."

Pero lo que me dijo me ha desconcertado desde.

But what he told me has bothered me since.

———

At a conference, years later, not too long before I watch *Arrival*, I hear Lee Maracle speak. She is writing a new book. She wants to know who among us have histories in places where English is not the majority language, as it has become here in Toronto. She asks how many of us don't speak our inheritance. About half the attendants raise a hand. She says she asks this to help explain what her book is about.

In the book, a time traveller goes a great distance, and at great hardship, to arrive at a particular time and place. He meets two small animals when he arrives.

"There's two minks in this little bush staring at him," she says in an interview about the book a few months later, "and he says, 'Is this Tkaronto?' And they start laughing at him. 'Tkaronto? That's Mohawk, man. Nobody talks that anymore! Not even the Mohawks speak Mohawk!' and they just kill themselves laughing at him. And he can't figure out how they could not speak their language, so he starts panicking. 'Okay, okay, some of them speak Mohawk. But nobody says Tkaronto, they say Toronto. Torawnna.'"

The time traveller is distressed at this loss. "Your reso-nators, your lips, your tongue, your whole body, your very cells are shaped for this language," she says.

And so, she asks us: How does it feel to not be able to

communicate with your own body? To not be able to speak with yourself?

"What I'm hoping is that people will get that they have to know their original language," she says in that interview. "And I think that's why the Six Nations have a constitution that guarantees you your original language. And it's a thousand years old. So for a thousand years we've known this. That the body speaks to itself. And it speaks the original language. It won't give it up."

This idea calms me. It doesn't immediately dawn on me that what I'd consider my original language embodies its own fracture with history.

My first expressions of love communicated to you in human language were "M'ijo, mi amor." And then: "It's you."

Birth and memory are mischievous cousins who like to play tricks, though, so while I do remember speaking them in this order, I don't know for sure. But I'm glad if I did. It felt good for me to speak to you in this language while I was pregnant.

I sometimes say *mira* because I want you to look, and you do not need me to point to know what I mean. I say *vamos*, and we get going. I say *aiee no*, in that particular, satisfying whine that is more Mexican than Spanish, when rushing towards the site of some small non-emergency: overturned chairs, a food fight, your brother reaching to unplug a precariously placed lamp.

Right now, I know you understand me either way. It's the form—the language the words come in—that would send you into a rage from time to time when you were little. I'd read you bilingual picture books; sing songs I remembered from childhood. You hated them. "Speak normal!" you'd insist. I remember the Saturday mornings my mother dragged me out of bed for Spanish school; I resisted those, too.

I can't know what the experience of sharing a body was like for you, just as I can't know for sure what you take from either language when I use it. But some things are givens. That I once pumped blood into your growing body. For a while, you would bump into my ribs, kidneys, and hip bones with spells of hiccups. There is a lilt to Spanish, and when you cried as an infant, that made it easier for me to tell you: "Please don't cry, I love you—and please don't cry *because* I love you." It comes through in the elongated sounds of saying, "No llores, mi amor. No llores."

Spanish was the first language I was shown love in, and I don't think I began to understand this until I had another way of speaking to show me the difference.

—

After watching *Arrival* I came to trust language less. Or, more specifically, the idea that the nature of what you speak structures the nature of your knowledge.

In grade school I was taught that the Tower of Babel was a curse story, that the confusion that follows from giving people different ways of speaking was God's divine punishment for human ego. Then, in later years, something that debunked that earlier xenophobic idea: that linguistic diversity can mean a variety of ways of knowing are possible.

We are taught that the way we speak determines the way we experience and think about the world; that words aren't the containers for our knowledge so much as the nature of the knowledge itself. This is meant to be encouraging. The more languages, the more ways to understand one another, the better we all get along.

As a film, *Arrival* hinges on the Sapir-Whorf theory of linguistic relativity, a hypothesis generally accepted in principle but whose underpinning research is troubled by Western scholarship's tendency to rely on Indigenous languages to confirm preconceived notions about the people speaking those languages of study. Working after his mentor Edward Sapir's death in 1939, Benjamin Lee Whorf took a particular interest in Hopi, an Uto-Aztecan language spoken by the sovereign nation of people who live in what's now known as northeastern Arizona. His interpretation of how time is used—or, in his view, not used—in the language led him to believe that the Hopi perceive time differently, an argument that pop culture somehow transmogrified into the idea that Hopi culture does not have a concept of time at all. An argument that has since been thoroughly disproven.

Despite being heavily informed by linguistics, it's notable that in Chiang's story, which *Arrival* is based on, the Sapir-Whorf hypothesis isn't mentioned once. But a good deal of dialogue focuses on explaining Fermat's principle of least time, which suggests that the path a light beam takes is the fastest one regardless of the medium it moves though—air or water or gas or otherwise. This principle, theorized well before physicists better understood the properties of light, seems troublesome at first. The idea of *fastest* can only exist within parameters, and such a calculation is only possible if the location of point B in relation to point A is known in advance. It suggests that a beam of light already knows where it's going. As it relates to this story, not "known" in the anthropomorphic sense, but in a goal-based one: that light travelling through air changes direction once it plunges into water is not so much *caused* by the water as it is a means of faster arrival. The alien beings Louise learns to speak with see the world on these terms, and she comes to see it, too: once past, present, and future coexist, one acts, and feels, in terms of inevitability.

I was stunned when I read "Story of Your Life," well after watching the film adaptation. At its tone, pacing, and how the protagonist's daughter is written as a living, breathing human being, not the result of a choice. It is tempting upon first read to see this story as *Arrival* does: as Louise choosing to have a child despite a new language giving her the power to understand what will happen if she does. It is possible to understand why a screen-told story would need to take this path.

But as a text, "Story of Your Life" suggests something far quieter and more hopeful. Louise knows she will have her child, and has chosen to live as though she is putting one foot in front of the other always, despite her newfound ability to see her life in purely teleological terms. It's how she retains her humanity. It's how anyone might when confronted with circumstances that might otherwise give way to despair.

Louise describes life inside a language in which she can now think. "Usually, [this new language] affects just my memory: my consciousness crawls along as it did before, a glowing sliver crawling forward in time, the difference being that the ash of memory lies ahead as well as behind: there is no real combustion. But occasionally I have glimpses when [it] truly reigns, and I experience past and future all at once; my consciousness becomes a half-century-long ember burning outside time. I perceive—during those glimpses—that entire epoch as a simultaneity. It's a period encompassing the rest of my life, and the entirety of yours."

In inhabiting both, for Louise the past becomes as mutable as the future; specific memories take on new significance and become as vital as her present. The language isn't time travel, but it holds another power: it helps her make sense of her life. She is coming to terms with grief as she is living through the part that makes it worth it. She is rehearsing a story she knows she will never get to tell her daughter, even before she is born.

Anxiety, especially that of early parenthood, laced my mind to thinking solely in cause and effect. If *this*, then *that*. Over and over. But a few times since you were born, I have experienced that half-century-long ember burning outside of time, and I've been chasing it ever since. It gets easier. I'm on the streetcar with you and you're still in the stroller and we're on our way to the Eaton Centre, where I know the bathrooms have clean and functional change tables. I hear a woman speaking on the phone, presumably to a child. *Pórtense bien.* It translates to: Be good. It means instead: I'm going now. I love you.

I'm on the streetcar with you, but I'm not. I'm four years old and my mother is putting me to bed; she makes a sign of the cross on my forehead the same way she will sometimes do for her grandchildren thirty years later. I'm sixteen and on the phone with my aunt while she paints her nails, and I feel like I'm speaking through a sieve. I'm twenty-eight and hugging family goodbye in the cement courtyard in the house in Vallarta with the peach and white bougainvillea in bloom and I'm pregnant and do not yet know it. You're two years old and I'm reading the Spanish translation of *A Color of His Own*, a board book about a chameleon who just wants to remain one colour forever, and you pluck it out of my hands. You're sixteen, and you call me for some reason or another; you're going to be out late, I need to sign some kind of form, you forgot your keys at home. Or maybe thirty-six, as old as I am now, and you're calling again, from some other place, some other time. What version of your life will you have dreamed up by then?

I DON'T RECALL EXACTLY when he said this, but one evening while flipping through childhood photographs, your father pointed at a picture of himself at a year old: soft, happy, and drooling in a pill-yellow sweatshirt. "This is Fa's daddy," he said with conviction, a proud emphasis on the *this*. He meant the gesture as a kind of disbelief at being a parent, the seemingly impossible connection to be drawn between the child he remembered himself to be and the child he was responsible for now.

I understood the statement as literal. Not: *This baby will grow up to be a father to our son someday.* Nor: *Look at the human being I once was! Soft, happy, and drooling, like our son is now.*

Instead, the baby in the photo at once was, and is: a new parent; an impatient teenager who drinks from soda cans out of the side of his mouth so as not to obstruct or interrupt his reading; a music teacher in his late thirties who eats Kit Kat bars whole without snapping them into pieces because he loves the candy bar so much. I don't think of this as destiny, exactly, but maybe an acknowledgement that as much as your past shapes who you are as a parent, your experience of parenthood also reconfigures your past. This reconfiguration may happen multiple times; you may have to relearn the same lesson over and over again.

There is a word I often associate with this reality that isn't typically applied to parenthood, but is deeply linked with time. *Tigersprung*, the tiger's leap into the past, Walter Benjamin's contention that how art changes is not linear, but folded over and under itself a million times over, the way one weaves a length of cloth. Pull a thread in one direction: it betrays the fabric's structure, revealing how it is held together by a set of recurrences, patterns, the tiger leaping forwards through time at particular moments in the warp and weft to make itself known again. Perhaps this is what learning, relearning, practice, looks like. Perhaps parenthood is something like that.

THE FIRST TIME MY mother saw you, she shrieked with a delight I'd never heard before. For a moment, it frightened me. "He has my dimples!" she exclaimed. She isn't the kind of person to speak this way, especially not in English. It's not that my brother and I hadn't experienced this type of love from her. It's that I hadn't ever had the experience of seeing it from outside of its loop. Watching her rub your belly when it was new and full of gas; watching her pour water over your head with a cupped palm to bathe you when you were still small enough to fit in the sink. I was only just learning to do these things. In showing me, I could see her remembering past versions of herself.

I see these things and think about the young woman my mother was while bathing my brother and me. Sometimes I assume that in those moments, she had the same confidence, the same assured technique of gently dribbling water over the rounds of an infant's head and stomach from a squeezed washcloth, even though I know that's likely a fiction.

I wonder how much of her joy now is wanting to relive that time in her life, to be close to feeling promise again, with the lived assurance that some things, at least, will turn out just fine.

YOU WERE BORN ON New Year's Day. I lit a candle the evening we brought you home because we didn't have a night light and I wanted to watch you breathe; to be sure of what it sounded like, to be sure you were still doing it. If I'd heard a baby breathe before, I didn't know it then. You were sluggish and moved so little in utero in the weeks beforehand that I drank a glass of ice water most evenings just to feel you kick. It's a miracle this paranoid habit hasn't left your feet cold.

In *The Argonauts*, Maggie Nelson says that "to let the baby out, you have to be willing to go to pieces." This proved harder for me to do in the weeks that followed the passage of birth. I was prescribed bedrest; I couldn't leave dirty dishes in the sink. I spent weeks recording the length of every nursing session, the weight of supplementary bottles, the number and timing of diapers in a day. For a few months I pumped milk, dozens of plastic bags in the freezer labelled with dates in neat, tiny print, to ensure you'd be fed on any occasion when I wasn't around or well enough to nurse you myself. It seemed a type of life insurance.

I didn't sleep more than four consecutive hours at a time for almost a year, and started spending your naptimes on my phone, scrolling through trading apps for things I didn't need and had no interest in acquiring. Snow boots. Skin serums. Bottle warmers. Then, one day, an heirloom: a bread starter for biscuits.

The woman offering the sourdough for trade indicated she'd inherited it from her grandmother and had fed it every week for years. A quiet glass pot of oat-coloured froth that asked only to be fed flour, water, and sugar every seven days, instead of nursed every three hours on an endless clock. The connection, I realize now, is ludicrous, but my brain leapt there immediately. Was it sleep deprivation? Fear of failure? I messaged the woman at once. In exchange for two cups of starter, she asked for lip balm.

We are parents to very few things that become our food. There's livestock, yes, if you eat meat and raise the animals, but no matter how tenderly a farmer feeds her pigs or grooms her cows, she's still tending to a one-sided relationship. No matter how hard the work, the bacon is simply for her benefit.

Horticulture comes closer. An ear of corn's juicy snap wouldn't exist if not for nine thousand years of selective breeding. By means of economy or colonial violence, often both, we have arranged ourselves—entire cuisines, traditions, and trade systems—around this crop that once grew on its own as potato-flavoured grass. But as an analogy, this too has its limits. Both arrangements, animal and crop, expect that the caregiver will outlive the immediate ward; it's almost entirely the point.

Newly, there was a baby in my home, and newly, four mothers. One human—the one I became—and the rest bacterial colonies mixed with cellulose and yeast that would float in jars like pearly blobs of fat, starter cultures for sourdough bread and kombucha, which I also acquired in those first few months. Even from a technical perspective they couldn't rightly be called "mothers," in the sense of procreators of offspring. But they were, in a general sense, progeny-makers, ones that needed a bit of care in order to produce. I thought about this often, usually when clipping your toenails, noticing the silk of your hair turn colours, or checking a new jar of fermenting tea for fresh fizz—a sign that it's ready to drink.

In *Ongoingness*, Sarah Manguso describes a kind of falling away from the obsessive need to document every detail of every waking moment of her life once she had a child. For one, she simply didn't have the time. The larger reasons are, I have come to realize, a little more counterintuitive to mainstream experience.

Like it did for many parents, or at least like it did for me, the arrival of a child restructured Manguso's experience of time: its passage, its many valuations, and her expectations around its use as a measurement of growth as a person.

For many new parents, the reaction to this transformation is to feel like every waking moment requires a pause, a photograph, a video shot by phone, a text to a partner at work, because the happy wounds of that fresh reordering of time make it seem like such a heartbreak to let the endless pattern of diaper changes and feedings rob you of every gurgle or startled smile.

For Manguso, it was the exact opposite. Delighting in and giving herself over to the experience of caring for another human being meant that she was precisely where she was meant to be at any given moment, even when it came to her work as a writer, and even if she wasn't writing about her son explicitly. I try to remind myself of this when I feel guilty that my husband finds the time to make new pictures of you, and has amassed an archive of photographs that far outweighs my own.

I think instead about the early, embodied record of having cared for you and your brother: the way one of my ribs still clicks from months of nursing hunched over; the way I've memorized the unique pattern of each of your barefooted gaits on the floor; the similar way your heads would shiver in disgust at certain foods as infants. In the future, these details won't be of much use to you the way photographs might be; I think about how I will describe them.

There are things I never recorded that I'm worried will fade—things I have little language for. There isn't a word, for example, for the first few months of an infant's life, when so much about their countenance seems to be expressed as a question. Everything about you at this time was always searching. For a face to look at, for something to wrap your new fingers around, for your own hands, own mouth, anything. Clasping and unclasping hands as practice. Open? Closed. Open? Even your breath—soft milky sour, a curly smell—was asking.

There is a sound you made while nursing that explains this better. A repeated sigh, an upwards slide, usually in the last moments of a feed, just before falling asleep. An unarticulated question that did not need an answer.

———

For a while, listening to the high-pitched twinkle of music made for infants was unbearable. I was often scared to acknowledge that it made me think of endings, limits, sometimes even death.

Hearing the ascending leaps of "Tomorrow" from this ceramic Peter Rabbit music box my husband had as a child only made me feel worse after so many failed attempts at nursing, and feeling both that I couldn't provide for you and that you, coming to realize it, were utterly devastated by that knowledge.

This was even after I spent nearly an hour holding you naked on my skin, calming you down, and letting your father convince me this fear wasn't fact. Hearing that melody made me feel stupid.

In the first two weeks after you were born, your father played two albums on a near-constant loop: Steve Gadd, and *Wincing the Night Away* by the Shins. Why these albums specifically? There are certain songs that I've now come to associate with a feeling I did not yet have words for, a mix of being hurt by something beautiful, anticipation, fear, gratitude. It was the beginning of a kind of love I wasn't familiar with.

The feeling these albums and certain images flash-bulbed into memory: watching your father awkwardly hold you, not yet the length of a forearm, in his hands for the first time. Watching smiles flicker across your face while you slept in the yellow glow of the lamp we got to replace that candle after dark. Rubbing your father's slouched shoulders and pressing my face into his hunched back while he rocked you to sleep. Feeling the crest of a beginning, of something overwhelming, though not yet knowing what that thing was, and also feeling afraid that beginnings of things don't exist without ends.

I spent many hours, late at night, scrolling through message boards and resource sites dedicated to teaching those new to the work of nursing the difference between foremilk and hindmilk, the feeling of a let-down, the sound of a well-latched baby's swallow. You were sleeping contentedly in the bassinet on one side of the bed, your father softly snoring on the other. There was no reason to be awake.

The ontology of food-based bacterial cultures lies somewhere along the porous boundary between sustained life and arrested death—or fermentation and decomposition, as the case may be.

The functional reasoning for all this: to make what's fresh last longer; to control the life of what nourishes us by stretching the boundaries of its expiration. In less savoury terms, the sour hum of kimchi is rotting cabbage coated in salt and spice; a ripe raw-milk Camembert is stirred with bacteria genetically similar to what's found in our armpits and between our toes, left to coagulate, aged, then rinsed in mould. My favourite understanding of this comes from Noella Marcellino, a Benedictine nun who has a Ph.D. in microbiology and sees the divine in rot. "You don't really want to talk about what cheese reminds you of," she told Michael Pollan in a Netflix documentary. "It's this sense that we're eating decomposition, breakdown products. You could call it death. To me, it's a taste of that, but a promise of something delicious."

Bacteria can also taste alive: a bright, bubbly sourness informed by hundreds of cycles of brewing, proofing, and the yeasts that happened to be hanging around the locale of production. Perhaps this is what inheritance tastes like, and explains why continuously fermented foods are expressed through language and ideas also used to talk about family, in the biological and the sociological sense. A kombucha culture—a gelatinous disc of yeast and bacteria that ferments sweetened tea into a tart, fizzy drink—can be a mother or a baby; the culture produces a new layer of cellulose with each brewing cycle. There are food-based bacterial cultures that date back generations. The trademark tang of Boudin Bakery's bread in San Francisco is credited to a sourdough starter nearly 170 years old, and some ardent home bakers will pass on prized starters to their children. A mole sauce can exist indefinitely, with a bit of the earlier batch fed into the new one every time it's remade, the DNA of its flavour transforming from week to week.

The baker or brewer doesn't live off bread or tea alone, of course, but this does get closer to something resembling a reciprocal relationship.

The day a healing crack in my nipple reopened and bled from nursing, or I rocked you for two hours in front of our apartment's front door because the wind that blew through the frame's cracks was the only thing that put you to sleep. The day I lifted your feet a little too high while changing your diaper and you urinated in your own mouth. The day I woke up in bed hunched over, convinced I was holding you, then convinced I dropped you, then confused to find you sleeping in the bassinet, where you'd been all along. This happened more than once.

On the painful days, and the stupid ones, I'd scoop out a dollop of the starter, mix it with milk, flour, cheese, and salt, and drop it onto a baking sheet with a spoon. Cheese rolls. Or skip the cheese, double the milk, and pour it into a hot pan for pancakes. Sometimes these efforts did not end well—hockey-puck pretzels or crepes that pulled apart like two-ply tissue—but this was fine, too. Small triumphs on days I'd forgotten to shower were comforting, while the failures felt safe. No one was going to grow up maladjusted and angry just because I'd made a shitty waffle.

Diapers and laundry aside, much of the early work of first parenthood, for me, was relearning how to arrive at knowledge through observation—and learning when to trust that such knowledge is enough. There are, I realize, many other ways of living that demand this skill, but those sleep-deleted weeks offered no respite from the terror of not knowing. *How do I know my child has nursed to fullness? What is that little twitch he does when he sleeps? Does an orange skid mark in his diaper count as a full bowel movement? What will happen if I don't dry the skin properly between the soft rolls of his chin and his little neck? How do I know that he's well, thriving, alive? How do I know he will outlive me?*

One thing I love about many types of guardianship in food is that it requires you to observe, but not too closely. There is no interior magic in watching a blossom become a peach. Follow a set of instructions and you can keep a bread starter healthy and productive for years.

I used to think this watching wasn't possible with pregnancy, with self-improvement, and for a little while after giving birth, with being a parent, too. That either the diligence required—the counting, measuring, endless questions, and self-doubt—would render you inert, or you could submerge yourself in the participation so fully that remembering how you got anywhere was just a series of disconnected blinks. And so, in many aspects of my life, I've simply committed to one or the other, seeing them as mutually exclusive approaches to love. I still don't know how to do both at the same time, but I am learning.

Sometime after I brought the first bread starter home, I lost the photocopied piece of paper listing the feeding ratios that had accompanied it. And then, one day—perhaps it was a painful day, or a stupid one—I pushed the little glass jar to the back of the fridge and forgot about it for a few weeks. When I eventually remembered it and pulled it out of the fridge, the starter, usually bright and tangy with a tart smell, had retreated into itself and developed a runny brown liquid that reeked of spilled alcohol—a sign, internet searches informed me, that the bacteria and yeasts that comprised it were hungry. I was certain I'd killed it. I wasn't heartbroken, but I was too attached to the greying little blob to throw it in the trash. So, I guessed the best I could, mixed in the flour, water, and sugar, and left it on the counter for a while. In less than a day, it began to bubble.

The first day I returned to work after my first child was born was the last day I nursed him. I hadn't planned this symmetry, but I had suspected its imminent arrival for a few weeks. He'd taken to tracing the bridge of my nose when I rocked him to sleep, and this brought him more comfort than nursing. I'd made up a simple melody for "The Owl and the Pussy-Cat" and turned it into a lullaby, and he asked for it often. It predictably sent him drifting off to sleep each night. He never had to ask for nursing that was denied him. He'd weaned without tears. It felt like the best work of my life.

I woke up that morning when he called for us at five, and brought him to our bed. He fed for maybe five minutes, sat up, and shook his head. "No." *Ah! Okay then.*

In part because of a habit of understanding concepts such as growth and progress as neat little units that click into place, rather than ongoing projects, this seemed like fortuitous timing. I clung to the idea of a year and assigned it all sorts of meanings and responsibilities. A year to figure out how to teach him to sleep through the night, to eat well, to be comfortable in the company of other caregivers.

A year to learn how to handle work, school, and family responsibilities on the same twenty-four-hour clock. A year to perfect the job of parenting, as if parenting was ever anything other than constant adaptation.

I transitioned out of parental leave the way one might progress from one school grade to the next. I'd ticked off the boxes, passed all the tests I'd set up for myself. It was time to return to the public broadcaster where I worked and to set up a whole new list to check off.

For the first few days, this is exactly what it felt like. On my first day back at work, I jumped out of bed at 5:30 a.m. to pack a lunch, shower, and dress before he woke up. This gave me an uninterrupted hour with him before I left for the office, where I was eager to do everything that nap schedules didn't allow for. Extended conversations with colleagues about industry gossip, politics. Having time to think about a single idea for more than ten minutes. The deep and previously unappreciated pleasure of finishing a mug of coffee while still hot. The naive belief I could do all this and still spend what felt like enough time with my family. It lasted for two weeks at most.

By the end of the first month, the predawn routines were out the window. There were some nights my son would wake up and start chatting through the baby monitor to anyone who'd listen, excited about some new motion he wanted to repeat or word he had learned to say. By the end of the second month, prepacked lunches consisted of whatever in the fridge could be forced into a Ziploc bag; any further planning seemed a pointless luxury.

In March, the daycare germs hit. Endless runny-nose colds filled the bathroom wastebaskets with soggy tissues, and eventually we were visited by fifth disease, a milder cousin to rubella and measles that still has all the aesthetic markings of a biblical affliction. High temperatures, copious vomiting, and a lacy red rash I'd never before seen on human skin, until it was on his—and then on mine, too.

It was at some point in the middle of that feverish week that I kept thinking: at this same time the previous year, I'd just gotten comfortable with nursing. Naps had taken on a pattern. I could swaddle him with ease; disassemble and disinfect breast pump equipment in a five-minute routine. I was becoming more confident in the role and label of *parent*. How could things be moving backwards?

THE FIRST TIME THE young girl notices her mother is getting ready to leave for work, it is early evening. The mother has just given her and her baby brother a bath. She has blow-dried the children's hair and rubbed cream into their arms and legs, pounding the base of the nearly hollow lotion bottle against the palm of her hand to get every last drop out. Nothing goes to waste, including time: during bathtime, the mother's hair has been setting in rollers and her outfit is laid out.

It was blue.

Was it?

Yes, a blue skirt. You had blue eyeshadow, too.

That was my makeup case. But the eyeshadow might have been blue, yes.

Why did you work at night, Mom?

So I could be at home with you during the day. I didn't have much of a choice back then.

ONE AFTERNOON, YEARS BEFORE I became a mother, my friend Carolyn picked me up from Keele Station with her two children, then three years and six months old, strapped into the back seat. We'd gone to school and worked together, and given that she was older than me when such blocks of time seemed significant, the order and pace of her life made sense, looking at it from the outside. I hadn't seen her since her daughter was born, and it was raining heavily.

"What were we talking about?"

I don't remember what we greeted each other with, but I remember her expression, one hand on the steering wheel and her palm against her temple. "Something happens to your brain after having kids," she said. "You can't *think*." The clarity of this memory, even today, is striking. The rain evenly pouring down the windshield, the smell of zinc in the car, her voice, the curl of her daughter's hair. It's likely the quality of her frustration—completely new to me then, though I later identified with it daily for almost five years—has affected its encoding and recall.

I'd think of this moment when I poured cumin into the oatmeal instead of cinnamon; when I'd momentarily forget the names of celebrities, co-workers, mix up the names of my own children; when I'd put on my shoes to leave the house and feel the crunch of a tiny palmful of Cheerios inside. It would unspool itself across my mind like a never-ending ticker tape. *You can't think. You can't think.* Sometimes: *You'll never think again.*

Whenever this happened, I'd fruitlessly try to contain it, as if winding the tape back up were possible. Something about health journals' exhortations to new mothers to be kind to themselves—that calling the grey-matter loss during pregnancy and new parenthood, an empirically measurable phenomenon, "mom brain"—felt patronizing. Slightly insulting, even. For all the aspects of perinatal health that have been left uninvestigated, ignored, and deemed unimportant, scientific proof of why it is normal to feel less capable and slightly insane after giving birth was supposed to be a reassurance?

At the same time, performing the machinations of a public working life as though I was unfettered by parenthood felt dishonest. Participate too fully in your life without your children and you are failing at motherhood; jump into your life as a mother and fail to remain the person you were beforehand, and you are no longer a whole person. You are sitting atop the cake of the culture; be grateful. Do not complain about the flavour of the frosting, as Maggie Nelson writes. Do not ever suggest you enjoy the cake too much. There is, I learned quickly, a line to walk that displays a specific level of both satisfaction and dissatisfaction with contemporary motherhood.

I wrote about new parenthood—new motherhood specifically—in a way the culture rewarded then: how motherhood made me *feel*, to the exclusion of asking why, or how, these feelings and their causes related to the world around me. Losing a pregnancy broke me a little; giving birth broke me a little; learning to nurse broke me a little; learning to return to myself after becoming a mother broke me a little. To become a mother, at least on the page, one must fall apart—but only a little, never completely. All the better if this damage is somehow consumable. The post-aughts decade ushered in shelves upon shelves of new-mother memoirs—many written in tight, spare language indicative of the fragmentation of time and memory involved in raising small children. Possible to write, and therefore read, between naps and feeding and paid work. I inhaled as many as I could find. They felt nourishing.

A few weeks after our household recovered from fifth disease, I flipped through our streaming service for something fun to watch and landed upon *Workin' Moms*, a scripted CBC comedy series about the lives of five women adjusting to parenthood in a new mothers' group. In the first season, the lead character struggles with balancing a return to work as an executive at a PR firm and living up to her ideals of what a mother should be. By the second episode, she has fired the nanny, who is conveniently written as an incompetent, obstinate Filipina caregiver who insists on bringing her dog to work. (The crime: feeding her breastfed child infant formula, something no childcare worker in this day and age would *dream* of doing without explicit permission, for this very reason.) From family members to hired help, no caregiver is trustworthy; though most members of this mums' group constantly ridicule the sole woman who'd prefer to take care of her child full-time. There is an extended scene with a Rubik's Cube of a very expensive foldable stroller. There are right ways to suffer as a mother, its ethos suggests, and contemptible ones too. I stopped watching after the first season.

Motherhood as subject, motherhood as genre. While understanding motherhood this way can spotlight stories our culture is often eager to ignore, a genre is easy to pigeonhole; a subject too prone to being spoken about in absolutes about an experience that is not necessary universal. It hadn't yet occurred to me that motherhood could also be understood as structure, an organizing principle, infinitely interpretable.

MY HUSBAND THOUGHT FOR a while he might like to become a watchmaker. He had bought me a ring when we decided to get married. In return, I bought him his first wristwatch.

I was twenty-three, and trying very hard to pretend not to be. I misguidedly thought at the time that my qualms about the acquisitive and inequitable nature of state-sanctioned marriage could be addressed, levelled out somehow, with equalizing measures that added up to yet more consumption. I'd won a small writing prize months earlier, and confidently walked into a jewellery store on Cumberland with my earnings, unsure of what I was looking for. I pointed to a stainless-steel Movado with polished square links that clicked together like little teeth.

My husband has always wanted to understand the world through movement. He picked up a guitar for the first time at nine; by his mid-teens he was sanding down pieces of wood to build instruments of his own. After he learned to drive, he thought he might build a car someday, and eventually did, but I gave him the watch first, and in a moment of desperation about how music or car repair was going to earn him a living he looked at the Movado and asked himself *who made this?*

In doing so he became obsessed with the tiny machine, and with the value of measured time outside of a bar of music. From the Enlightenment onwards, every scientist, philosopher, and aristocrat in the Western world convinced themself they needed a working clock—in essence, to control time—in order to be *of* the world. In our current age, the measurement of time by physical movement has become a high-end product that pays dividends to those who know how to maintain its machines, of which there are fewer every year. When I gave my husband that first watch, luxury groups were clamouring for trained technicians who could wind, oil, and repair the instruments of the Enlightenment. But only one watchmaking school remained in Canada, far from where we lived, and taught in French only. He concentrated on teaching music instead.

Years later, in the early hours of my first labour, my husband was eager to put a watch to use. He recorded the time of every contraction with unnecessary specificity. And after the birth: every nursing session, bowel movement, diaper change, awakening. Pages and pages of numbers. We both thought a written record could provide information that my body and infant already had no trouble communicating. My breasts told me when I'd waited too long to feed the baby; the baby told me beforehand, sucking his fingers and turning his head. Once a night my husband fed him by bottle, using a warmer to heat up the milk. The timer cranked and clicked loudly, spelling out the seconds until he could quell his son's hunger. I often woke up to it. That warmer drove him insane.

"We'll all of us die from the madness of clocks." Marosia Castaldi's narrator repeats this over and over in *The Hunger of Women*, every time she hears her neighbour vacuuming the carpet. She fears the winding down of her life being measured by the high-pitched whine; in midlife and newly without children or a husband in the house, she is fretful about what her own life lived by the clock of domestic work might mean for whatever "scrap of eternity she might leave to the earth."

The machines of our maintenance have the power to undo us a little, I think. By our son's sixth week of life, my husband had learned to wake up a little earlier and run a hot tap over the bottle.

THE EDITOR'S WORK IS that of imagined non-presence—the translator's, too—as is the care and feeding of small children. The labour of each is an act of interpretation, communication, executed with care. I think beauty can be found in maintenance. I grate at the idea that it is not an art.

There is feeding. The spectrum of experience encompassed in nursing, from the first let-down to weaning, would overwhelm even the most acute observer of human nature. The fatigue, the ecstasy, the boredom, the endurance of pain, the anxiety in public space, the frustration, the slow and delicious creep of connection—seeing your child look you in the eyes for the first time while feeding, grasping your collarbone, poking fingers into your mouth. I felt this feeding my children by breast and by bottle; I'm not convinced I arrived at this knowledge by one method alone.

There is cleaning. Wiping every variety of bodily fluid, picking the seborrheic yellow flakes off a newborn's scalp, disassembling and cleaning a milk pump with the ease and precision of a machinist. Changing diapers where social infrastructure does not treat it as a public necessity: on makeshift tables, car trunks, sometimes with one hand in order to keep the baby still with the other. Spills, intentional and not; learning to catch vomit in a plastic bag, in your hands if need be. For a short while, your body becomes an instrument of two selves.

There is care, from the early hours of learning precisely what type of elliptical motion will calm a crying spell to navigating the nascent and increasingly complex emotional life of a child. Raising a child to feel safe, loved, and secure is—in addition to every high and low feeling it can incite, every bruise of a past wound it can press on—work.

The "ordinary devotion," as Donald Winnicott called it; the diligent love, the maintenance in raising a child. More common than we think, more difficult than anyone can prepare to experience for the first time.

"EVERYTHING I SAY IS Art is Art." Fifty-five years ago, New York artist Mierle Laderman Ukeles wrote this in *Manifesto for Maintenance Art, 1969!*, a document that laid bare her frustrations with the subsuming, identity-fracturing nature of maintaining a home and raising children while still wanting to make art as a woman on the cusp of the 1970s. So she made the work of her life at the time the work *of* her life. In a Duchamp-inspired sort of challenge to the interpreter, her labour became her art: every dish, diaper, and broom. "After the revolution, who's going to pick up the garbage on Monday morning?"

She made the ontological decision about what she defined as art in her manifesto, which used city-planning terminology to distinguish between development and maintenance as processes through which the world is made. Development: pure creation, individualized, public, (unsurprisingly) male. Maintenance: ensuring the conditions for creation remain right, communal, domestic—"Show your work—show it again."

The Whitney rejected the manifesto's proposal to stage a live-in exhibit, with Ukeles's daily work (the cleaning, dressing, cooking, and more), interviews with sanitation workers, and scientists processing deliveries of city refuse in real time on display for viewers. But the defining principles of her manifesto and proposal—that we are all maintenance workers of some kind, paid, recognized, valued, or not—would inform the rest of her career.

Ukeles went on to document through photographs how she cleaned a diaper, dressed her children, even washed the steps of public institutions. In her most recognized work, *Touch Sanitation*, she documented a year of meeting with more than 8,500 maintenance workers in the New York Sanitation Department, shaking their hands and thanking each one for "keeping New York City alive!"

In *Essential Labor*, Angela Garbes points out how "it's both remarkable—and damning—that Ukeles' message, unchanged over forty years, is as timely and relevant as ever." In the fall of the first year of the COVID-19 pandemic, vestiges of *Touch Sanitation* began to pop up all over the city as part of a new public installation: at subway stops, in Times Square, at the entrance of the Queens Museum.

Dear Service Worker, "Thank you for keeping NYC alive!" for —> forever . . .

Around this time, little heart-shaped neon lights began to pop up everywhere in Toronto. I'd walk around in the evenings and see them glowing from the windows of homes: pink, blue, purple badges of thanks to healthcare and other frontline workers, the product of a business that had pivoted from film lighting after the industry was put on hold. As the months and rolling lockdowns went on, nurses still went underpaid and overworked, classroom teachers remained embroiled in tense contract negotiations with the provincial government, and countless women continued with their newly rearranged lives and careers, some of which were stopped short due to changing childcare realities. These days, you can still spot one every so often, their soft light shining against the glass.

HE IS MY FINEST work. In Nikyatu Jusu's 2022 horror film *Nanny*, an undocumented newcomer caring for a New York couple's young daughter says this to a friend at a salon about her six-year-old son, waiting in Senegal to join her. The words caught me when I heard them in the theatre the first time. How lovingly imbued with a caregiver's understanding that *mother* has always been more verb than noun—and that such a verb is not relegated to the realm of mothers alone.

The working mother, as the world understands that term now, is an erasure twice over. There is the self-abnegating fiction of turning the word *mother* into a subject as opposed to a verb, and defining *work* as leaving home to earn a wage. The feeding, cleaning, and emotional work of caring for one's own child in this definition is unwaged, does not measure up, does not compare—though the term implies she is either engaged in this work as well, or is responsible for managing the hired labour that makes her existence as a working mother possible.

The fact of this hired labour is the second erasure. The term *working mother* came into popular usage in the seventies and eighties as a generation of largely white, middle-class women in North America secured post-secondary education and white-collar work. But so long as someone can be counted on, hired, or compelled to provide the milk, wipe the excrement, carry a child through the types of days that feel like years, mothers have been working, whether paid or not, whether given the choice to or not, whether they are even the child's mother or not.

In 1955, a hundred women from Jamaica, Barbados, and Trinidad migrated to Canada through a new labour program that opened up immigration visas to women in English-speaking Caribbean countries specifically for the purpose of performing domestic work. Until then, immigration policy had actively excluded people from these countries, but white middle-class women in Canada were entering the public workforce in greater numbers and there was a need. Through the West Indian Domestic Scheme, as it was called, single women aged 18–35 were allowed entry into Canada to work as live-in household help. After a year of keeping house and providing childcare, participants were granted landed immigrant status. After five years, a pathway to citizenship.

This experiment in managing a society's reproductive labour through immigration policy ended up lasting twelve years. The three thousand women who took part in the program facilitated the country's gendered shift in workforce demographics and built the foundation of Black Caribbean communities in Canada today. It came at a cost, however: these women were frequently subjected to hostile and racist working conditions and unimaginably long hours. Since their employment was tied to a household, they were often isolated. Finding work outside of the domestic category proved significantly difficult.

The federal government officially ended the program in January 1968, but continued to issue temporary visas for domestic work—notably with more stringent terms for pathways to citizenship. While the policies and programs have changed over the years, the structural effect remains the same today. Canada continues to rely on racialized migrant labour for care work, for both children and the elderly. This workforce—overwhelmingly women, and for the past couple of decades largely from the Philippines—is still subject to exploitation.

The legacy of temporary foreign work permits in Canada has since extended to other industries, often with their own attendant histories of abuse and exploitation. Once concentrated in agriculture, healthcare, and care work, use of these permits has since shifted towards the retail and food service sectors. Cashiers, cooks, and hotel lobby clerks work here for months at a time with no path to citizenship and little pay. One of the country's largest fast-food chains, a vendor of doughnuts, hockey nostalgia, and manufactured national identity, makes extensive use of this program.

The work that makes the world we enjoy possible will always be rendered invisible. We say this of people involved in service work; it's more true of those whose service is treated as temporary, disposable. We say this of mothers; it's more true of the act of mothering.

The summer after you were born I took the bus home from some errand or another, a solo commute that started out feeling spacious, not empty, and I remember it specifically because of the distinction. It was humid, so I wore shorts to feel the thick air on my legs. There was late afternoon light. I carried my wallet and nothing else, when usually I don't leave home without at least one more thing than is necessary. This habit doesn't come from imagining what might be possible or anticipating the unexpected, but is a necessity from within; I need to *feel* prepared, even if I often hinder myself in the pursuit of that assurance.

For example, when you were six days old, I took you to a nearby clinic for a hearing test—a four-block walk that also happened to be our first outing alone together, maybe all of thirty minutes. Here is what I packed: a blanket, a changing pad, three diapers, wipes, eczema cream, an extra onesie, a bottle of expressed breast milk, and a bottle of purified water with a single-serving packet of powdered infant formula, just in case.

"The muchness of her!" Alexandra Kimball notes of a new mother from a park bench while awaiting an appointment. "With a stroller ahead of her, a swollen knapsack on her back, and the child attached to her hand, she spread across almost the entire sidewalk, fore and aft, a whole ecosystem." In *The Seed*, she is writing about infertility; she also clocks in the book's first few pages the way the objects of new motherhood have the look and feel of grounding a person to the earth.

I hadn't yet figured out nursing, certainly did not know how to do so in public, and I keenly felt how much physical space my material assurance against these fears took up. Messenger bags, strollers, baby carriers—a mental packing list for it all.

This would have delighted you as a toddler, when your little red backpack matched mine. You'd list the things it contained, or the things it lacked, before we'd take lunch to the park or head out for groceries. Kleenex. Pull-Ups. An extra pair of shorts. You'd insist on zipping up the backpack and slinging it over your own shoulders. On carrying it yourself, even when it was sometimes too heavy. *Fa do it. Only Fa.* I'd think: *Are you learning to be like me? Were you born to be?*

When I got on the bus that afternoon, I didn't have to do the mental math of asserting space. Of trying to figure out where the stroller would fit, or how I'd deal with passengers irked by the inconvenience. An earlier version of me might have considered the many reasons, unrelated to parenthood, why a person would do a similar calculation. I just thought I felt free.

Spacious; not empty. The former is reserved for the backyards your grandparents kept, small seas of lawn tightly mown around overgrown raspberry bushes, drooping tendrils of bleeding hearts, and a little vegetable patch that sometimes popped out a small gnarled carrot or two. I loved and mythologized these plants precisely because of the kept distance between them. I was able to do so because I could sit in front of them, unbothered by soil or plants or grass; just lawn. Those early gardens your grandparents kept seemed more like museums. Whether it was because they loved this aesthetic or were playing at expectations they felt were put upon newly upwardly mobile suburban immigrants, they were good at it.

The latter is defined by absence. A lanced abscess. Something snatched out of a pair of gripped hands. A tree that grows in curlicues around a chain-link fence. Remove the obstruction, and its structure—the shape used to growing around it—sometimes persists. This is not necessarily a triumph.

I got on the bus; I sat down.

"Hey."

I was going home; I felt good.

"*Hey.*"

Yes?

"Do you like ice cream?"

Huh?

A man sitting across from me leaned forward. "You eat a lot of ice cream. I can tell. Your teeth are so white."

His features, meanwhile, were so delicate. Upturned nose, high cheekbones, little Nicorette teeth. Perhaps this was the reason for everything else: the shaved head, the lace-up boots, the German shepherd sleeping in a pile beside him. A tight scar pulled at the skin along one side of his neck up to his ear. His skin was starting to purple. He wanted to know where I was going. He wanted to tell me about how his dog had helped him through some of the hardest times in his life. He wanted to know where I was from. No, where I was *really* from. Or actually, wait, I shouldn't tell him. He would guess.

That same summer we went to Mismaloya, a cove beach just south of where your grandmother grew up, made famous as the filming location for John Huston's *The Night of the Iguana* and now known as a restaurant and hotel centre. We watched the cold blue waterline crawl higher and higher up the sand till the waves reached the restaurants, pushing the plastic chairs and tables around. Twenty, ten, even five years earlier, the high tides didn't do this. But that didn't seem important in the moment.

A child had waded out too far into the water, and was waving his hands in the air. He had a full-body wetsuit on. He looked like a strong swimmer. Despite this, it was clear he was drowning. Someone at the restaurant pointed out the scene for the diners. While you grabbed at shrimp and grilled fish with fat little fists, we all turned to look.

Two men—family, maybe?—called out to him from the beach. A third, a server, ran into the wet sand, jumped into the water, and kicked his way along the tide, sideways, straight for the boy.

"No te metas en el agua," the server told the boy's family once he'd dragged him back to the beach. "Es peligroso."

The family didn't bother to thank him, and you kept scraping at the plates.

Sometimes I'd purposely make my heart sink, run through scenarios in my head. I'd lock the stroller at every intersection, every subway platform, imagining how best to dive in after you should something go wrong. When I was little, I watched the Pacific pick up your uncle at seven years old and drag him across a small hill of mollusc-covered rocks on that same beach, ripping a line through the skin on his back. It came to mind every time I brought you near the water on that visit, every time someone asked when I'd dip you in the ocean for the first time. You were five months old then; I waited till you were three.

The bus heaved to a stop. A young man in headphones, likely a teenager, hopped on and into a seat. The dog woke up; the ice cream man sneered.

"Look," he said, to his dog, to me, or perhaps everyone on the vehicle. "Look at those pants. What a fuckin' disgrace." It was clear that it was not what the teenager was wearing was that really bothering the ice cream man.

"*Look.*" He nudged the dog with his boot, kickstarting a gurgling noise that eventually turned to a growl.

———

Should I be afraid? It was hard to know the answer to that question, and easy to believe an answer was something I needed to have.

I wrote that once, for a parenting magazine, about a specific decision your father and I made about your health shortly after you were born. Perhaps it best described more generally the rush to master the presence of you. The belief that such a thing was possible. In the first few months of your life, I worried about whether or not I was capable of keeping you alive, despite knowing that the odds were tipped towards me in that regard: we always had a home, always had work, always had family nearby. No one ever questioned our right to be together, a family, parents of a child, to live on the land that we did and still do.

So much of our current environment asks us to parent from a place of fear. The systems of power that render the world's inequalities material often benefit from this. Fear that you might forever hinder your child's health if you do not put the rest of your life on hold to nurse them exclusively for the first six months of their life, even at the expense of your sanity. Fear that you have not purchased enough of or the right equipment to bathe, clothe, and transport them around in an environment full of threats. Of what will happen if you can't afford childcare. Fear that you are not enough, and that somehow a very specific set of choices can and will deliver you and your child into some velvet, end-game version of the future where there are no more risks.

I want you to know: this isn't a story about harassment. It's a story about absence. For a moment, when the ice cream man seemingly threatened to sic an animal on a teenager, I looked at the man, the dog, and then the street, as the vehicle's side doors opened up to it and the boy hopped off.

As I walked up to the bus driver (to do what, exactly? Little could have been of use by then), an elderly white woman with a tightly coiled perm and silk scarf a couple of seats up from us raised her voice.

"German shepherds are intelligent, you know. Such good judges of character."

I wasn't new to public displays of what makes this world ugly, the sad entanglements of what might make a person behave this way. I have learned, if imperfectly, to rebuff and question violence. But this bus ride—that woman's response to such a sordid string of events, some-how more wilfully violent than anything else about that interaction—curdled something in me.

A few years later, I would see a different version of it while holding a borrowed copy of *Second Place* and waiting for the bus. You had just started school; I was with your brother, who was happily napping in the red stroller. A man walked up to the bus stop to coo at the baby and ask the usual questions: *How old is he? Does he sleep well?* Then: *Do you breastfeed him? When will you feed him next? Can I see?*

The switch was so sudden I barely registered it as it was happening. Before the questions devolved further I removed myself and your brother and walked to another stop. Your brother, undisturbed this whole time, was still sleeping. I cracked open *Second Place.*

In the book's first few pages, Rachel Cusk's narrator meets, as she describes it, the devil on a train—a man who comes to represent this not because he is lewdly pursuing her in this public place, or because of the things he is saying, or anything else he does. It's that her inability to respond to the moment opens up something horrible in her. "It was like a contamination," her narrator writes to a friend. "It got into everything and turned it bad" . . . Fear gives way to vacancy, she writes. "Fear is a habit like any other, and habits kill what is essential in ourselves. I was left with a kind of blankness . . . from those years of being afraid."

I hadn't become prone to fear so much as prone to vacancy—to leaving parts of myself behind in the moments

I needed them most. Any solidity, any understanding of what makes it possible for a person to put one foot in front of the other without looking at the chaos swirling beneath the surface of things, would vanish for a minute, and for a long while afterwards the thrum of that chaos kept piercing through.

THE SUMMER AFTER YOUR brother was born, just before you started school, your pa called me in a type of panic I thought familiar.

I have bad news. Are you okay to hear it? It's *really* bad.

Yes, Dad, okay, please stop hedging and just tell me.

Someone at a family birthday party in Vallarta had fallen sick with COVID. Two weeks later, everyone else in attendance had it, too. Dozens of people, over three generations, were sick, and—due to reasons of access, misinformation, misunderstanding—not everyone was inoculated against the disease. Tío Memo, your grandmother's middle brother, had already been hospitalized and intubated, along with three cousins. Aunts, uncles, cousins, children: everyone else was ill at home, wheezing in their beds, barely able to move.

If it had always been somewhat visible how Vallarta was—is—a place upon a place upon another, the next three weeks shot through those layers, illuminating each one.

Public and semi-private hospitals were thrown into chaos that summer, overrun with people stricken by a new strain of the virus, the private facilities largely reserved for tourists and those who could afford such care. Hospital admission itself was not a guarantee; there simply was not space. People across the city scrambled to acquire home care equipment, oxygen tanks and tubes. Your grandmother scoured Facebook groups to secure a set for my grandmother and aunts to share.

For three horrible weeks, she called once a day for the two to three minutes my aunt could handle speaking, and then relayed the information to me by phone. One cousin had picked up a tank. Another, only eleven, was running chicken broth between the bedrooms. Another hospitalized. Then Mamá Parito, then Tía Ana. One by one, four family members were sent to hospital and, one by one, they were returned to family as ashes, picked up during scheduled appointments. Little warning, no logic, not a word of goodbye. I blinked for hours after each phone call.

THE SUMMER AFTER YOUR brother was born, Toronto felt flush. People rolled up their sleeves for the best new vaccine available, queued to dine at newly constructed sidewalk patios, admonished politicians about school closures and crumbling public transit, and filled up the theatres again. It felt grotesque to withdraw from the world, but I did, and I know that you felt this, despite any effort I made to prevent it.

Despite professional advice not to hide sadness from my children, I can say that I did so because of the oft-repeated adage about the quality of a mother's happiness determining whether her children will thrive. Summer was ending, school was starting; I tried to make every morning the same. Pancakes. Oatmeal. Sunny breakfast, early afternoons in the park. The truth is I tried to play normal because I could not translate this feeling, but you saw it anyway.

On occasion I spent hours in the nursing chair, unable to move, afraid I'd drop the baby. Some nights your father heard me say things that frightened him. One morning, you pulled at my hand to get me to sit down at the top of the stairs and picked at my face, massaging my temples and lifting my eyebrows with your thumbs. "Are you . . . another mama?" you asked, the question both warranted and terrifying.

I thought I had arrived at a place in my life of some kind of self-possession. An understanding that relating to the world by explaining myself too much was less an act of communication or communion and more an act of centring power, simply by obsessively defining my positionality to it.

But the summer after your brother was born, this was all my brain could do. When I wasn't around you, I could not speak to anyone without keeping words about death inside my mouth. *Yes my family, they're in Mexico you see, they all got sick and a lot of them died! One cousin is relying on Facebook to find a blood donor for an operation she needs and another may not walk again! My grandmother left this world flipped over on her stomach, unable to breathe and with her dentures taken out, because the healthcare system has gone to shit and no one knows what's going on. No, they weren't all vaccinated! It's complicated!*

One afternoon, while grocery shopping, I said a version of these words to an acquaintance who did not know me well enough to hear them. A few weeks later, I repeated them to my physician. They both gave me a similar sympathetic, slightly confused look. Humiliating. Infuriating. The break between where my mind lived and where I really was became unavoidable.

THERE IS MORE THAN one way to pay for something with your life. As an expression it's typically understood as a payment or price, specifically death: dying for a cause or death as a consequence of an unwise choice.

Fairy tales often mean to parent this way. *Do not eat the sweets you have not earned. Do not trust the woman who has come to replace your mother. Do not follow the strange animal into the woods.* To a child, death can often seem like the only way to stop time. Boredom might come close, yes, but it's also a form of escape—one that lays the groundwork for exercising the kind of imagination that will make you the person you grow up to be. You eventually come to learn that it is the opposite of death, and that it is essential.

Later on, the idea of a life as payment takes on another form: that your life is currency, and it is possible to spend it unwisely. Perhaps the ability to freely "spend" it at all suggests a degree of agency that anyone who has it is historically lucky to have. If you are truly lucky, your knowledge of this will not lead you to believe—lead you to worry—that what you do with the time you have can be objectively valued.

In the years immediately after you were born, I began to understand this phrase in the way a lot of contemporary literature about motherhood grapples with the concept. That paying with your life can mean forgoing the multitude of alternative futures you might otherwise have had, small deaths of another kind, something often understood in full only after the fact, not without varying flavours of wistfulness or regret.

But the time and labour involved in raising a child can also be seen as a willingly given gift. I don't think motherhood is the only way of experiencing this kind of payment; it's just often discussed this way. People make choices with this kind of cost every day. More often than not, these choices are made for them.

It took a while for me to understand the vanity in seeing this as a one-way transaction. Yes, the futures and oceans of time I might otherwise have had without children, even if these were things I knowingly gave up, were a kind of price. But your existence makes my life as a mother possible. Every facet: wanted, joyful, painful, and absurd. Setting your life in motion was the price ("Love set you going like a fat gold watch," indeed), and will continue to be long after I'm gone.

THE SUMMER AFTER YOUR brother was born, I learned to think of repetition as a form of return. It was necessary to be someone's clock; to get up every morning and make the oatmeal; to encourage you to select a book every evening before bed. "It's true what they say, that a baby gives you a reason to live," writes Rivka Galchen. I actively avoided thinking about her next observation, an inversion of the statement—that a reason to live renders death impermissible.

It was necessary to ask for help and, just as my grandmother did for her, my mother came to hold your brother, make you soup, let you brush her hair in the afternoons, even as she grieved herself. That summer, this grief manifested itself physically. Blood vessels burst at random all over her body, bruises bloomed along her arms, and her eyes often glinted red. She dreamed of her mother and her sisters, speaking to her in ways she couldn't understand. A purple cast appeared over the skin on her back.

She got biopsies. I was convinced she was dying. I thought I was going insane.

But we still woke up every morning. We made oatmeal. My mother and I became legible to each other through repetition.

EARLY IN HIS CAREER, the Mexican pop idol Juan Gabriel wrote "Amor Eterno," the cry of a loved one grieving a death. The words were his, but its entry into the world was not; the song was a gift to his close friend Rocío Dúrcal, who first performed it in 1984. It went on to become one of the most recognized ballads in Latine pop culture, played at memorials across the diaspora, and followed Gabriel and Dúrcal's careers for the rest of their lives.

While the song had emotional resonance for them both, it is also a strikingly accurate portrayal of the physical manifestation of grief. More than once the singer comments on their own face, on looking into the mirror, on being unrecognizable to themselves, on wanting to close their eyes forever. The endocrine and hormonal responses to the type of depression grief triggers can and do literally change your face, altering the skin's tone, texture, elasticity. For a short while, my eyes looked smaller, my vision felt bleak. Patches of eczema flickered across my eyelids.

When I was very little, I'd sometimes wake to music playing downstairs. Once or twice, I padded down to find my father listening to "Amor Eterno" in the kitchen with his eyes closed. It only occurred to me the summer after your brother was born how much he understood your grandmother's grief. He himself had lost his father, in another country, with no warning and few family members nearby, and no way to say goodbye or bury him. He was just sixteen.

I'VE BEEN THINKING ABOUT return as a form of reproduction. One story, told many times over, each one a little true.

How many times did I step off a plane, at great expense to my parents, and lift the brass knocker on the enormous wooden door to my grandmother's house? How else might a child interpret such a door but as a gateway to what, literally, was another place? The cement courtyard, baked peach and white bougainvillea, every year a new dog named Tomas or Muñeca or Mike. Electric green paletas, plastic bags of cut sugarcane, the elderly welder next door who let roosters strut among his equipment and metal scraps. Rainwater in the cobblestones that turned the dust to paste. The boy in the little shop at the corner who found ways to pinch pockets of fat on my body. Piñatas strung perilously high and still made of clay.

Springs, Christmases, once for so many weeks the school called to admonish my parents about my absence, once for a while after my brother was born, long enough that I did not respond to my mother when she arrived to collect me.

Before NAFTA, before Walmart, before the tiendas were all replaced with plastic red OXXO signs. At some point in the cement courtyard I solidified the memory of this place as a type of origin and left it undisturbed for years—the ease of an identity explained through these signifiers too comforting to interrogate and too valuable to my life in Canada to put down.

I reread Dionne Brand's words. I remember her speaking, though her writing, to Eduardo Galeano, he who was once "nostalgic for a country which doesn't yet exist on a map." Sometimes the desire to belong is strong enough to distort memories to make them fit.

Where are you from? My answer was a place that was made for me every time I arrived. It no longer exists, if it ever did at all.

"'FATHER' IS A HYPOTHESIS but 'mother' is a fact."

Dora, in Angela Carter's *Wise Children*, has just learned the woman who raised her may have been her biological mother all long. Not her grandmother, as she and her twin sister grew up believing, and the fact of this revelation is not without its own world-reordering poetry.

Dora and Nora Chance—twin nieces of a sometimes-actor who takes on the legal status of their father, and daughters of a high-profile theatre and film star who refuses to claim them—have grown up watching men lilt through life under the label of *father*. It is so easy for these men to do this, and difficult for the sisters to watch, until they learn to disentangle themselves from the societal expectation that they apologize for their existence—and instead live precisely how they like, making the art they want, sleeping where and with whom they please, dressing splendidly, loving and hating with equal abandon.

"What a joy it is to dance and sing!" Dora often says,

having struggled to gain acceptance and legitimacy as a midcentury stage artist in her own right. She is fundamentally light of heart, the kind of lightness that is hard-won and rare, though I likely wouldn't have clocked this when I first read the book in my early twenties and decided I preferred Carter's writing on fairy tales, pornography, and murder.

Carter did not know *Wise Children* would be her last book. She was diagnosed with lung cancer shortly before it was published and put aside a fledgling manuscript to set her affairs in order before the disease took her life at fifty-one, leaving behind her husband and eight-year-old son.

I understand the trouble with assigning meaning to a story after the telling and after the teller is gone. But that's the nature of carrying a story with you through an extended period of your life. It's difficult to read *Wise Children* now without thinking about Carter on motherhood, and how she wrote motherhood into the book through its elision. The Chance sisters' ability to parse the unstable nature of fatherhood is only possible through living life as though the nature of their relationship to their mother is a given; it is unimaginable that the woman who accepted the work of raising them might have refused a life of being called their mother.

When Carter's Dora calls mother a "fact," she is not speaking biologically or even in the corporeal sense. She means that we are born into a world that encourages, if not requires, us to return to the idea of *mother* for the rest of our lives in some way. In *The Autobiography of My Mother*, Jamaica Kincaid's narrator begins her story with the death of her mother at her own birth. Every thing that follows feels marked by this absence, from the day her father leaves her with his laundress to the emotional detachment she is required to keep intact to maintain her autonomy as a woman growing up in midcentury Dominica. It structures how the narrator, who goes nameless for part of the book, tells the story of herself to herself towards the end of her life.

We return to the idea of mother, over and over. Regardless of who mothered us or not, how they did it, if they were any good; the answers to those questions become the rubric by which we make sense of the world, an origin of its own.

There is real harm in assuming this is universally true, however. "Because mothers are seen as our point of entry into the world," writes Jacqueline Rose, "there is nothing easier than to make social deterioration look like something that it is the sacred duty of mothers to prevent." To foist responsibility for the quality of our future on mothers alone isn't just a cruel game they are set up to fail at, it blames mothers at the personal and the societal level. People do bad things because their mother did not teach them well enough; carry lifelong hurt from something their mother said or did; cannot live well because their mother did not provide a good enough life for them. What's wrong with the world? *Mommy issues*, a shorthand that at once builds a misogynist framework for seeing the world, compresses people's real pain into the butt of a joke, and conveniently removes mothers as people from the freedom and responsibility to be good and good enough for their children. *You must be perfect, and you will be doomed to fail regardless.*

But there is, I believe now, something generative in thinking about mothering as an act of translation, between mother and child, and between those who mother themselves. There are too many ways to exist as a mother to call it a universal experience; we are better off finding ways to make its many languages useful in order to understand each other.

I understand my mother's life with two young children better when I think about the specific way she used to make meatballs: pinched out of a sausage casing, opened with a knife, into little kumquats that cooked dense and quickly and went well with tomatoes and rice. *Salchichas* in Spanish. I did not have meatballs the way most people understand this dish—meaty, pillowy, with a bit of crunch—until I was maybe twelve.

In the first weeks of the pandemic, when the grocery stores all had lineups and people tried to stretch the contents of the fridge out longer, I did something similar. I found a pack of sausages in the freezer, thawed them, and pinched their contents into a hot pan with tomato sauce and black beans and corn and rice. A blanket of cheese went overtop and it got tossed in the oven. Though no one was going anywhere that evening, or for many afterwards, I was delighted at how quickly it came together, and I thought about how my mother would sometimes make this, bone-tired, after getting home from a long commute. But convenience alone wasn't why her meatballs had looked this way. "I was afraid of making you sick," she told me, sometime later. She always opted for smaller cuts of meat, cooked straight through to the centre. It was such a small, innocent thing, the way her anxieties about convenience cooking and food poisoning created this short-lived understanding of what I thought about meat. A short-lived fact, even, created through translation.

"IT SEEMS TO ME awfully unfair to my mother that I don't remember the first two years of my life," writes Jazmina Barrera, during what she calls the white nights of that first year of motherhood: the feeding, care, and emotional transformation that results from the work of maintenance. "Biology is so unkind to mothers, not allowing their children to recall the times we were closest to them."

As a child, I felt closest to my mother when she curled my eyelashes. I asked her often. She'd use the ridge of a fingernail against the pad of her thumb instead of a curler, gently pinching the lashes section by section. I can still hear the small scrape of it, hair on nail, if I want to; feel the slight pressure, gentle and expert.

Learning to carry you through the days of your first year of life—to feed you, to be your landscape, a clock—was among the most meaningful and physically demanding work of my life. This knowledge only makes me more certain that I don't need concrete memories of those earliest days of my own life to honour my mother's care. I feel it. Even if my life had turned out differently—without children, without you—I know I would still.

What would I like you to remember? What would you want to know?

One October afternoon, I took you to the movies for the first time. You had just started school and children were wearing masks to class. We wore them on the bus. At the theatre. We'd periodically pull them down to shove popcorn salad in our mouths, a specific ratio of popcorn to Smarties to Sour Patch Kids to Maltesers we'd made up together in the second winter of lockdowns. On the way home, you fell asleep in the seat on the bus and snored softly, the late afternoon sun slowly running over your purple sweater in patches of golden light.

I thought of the woman at the airport from years ago, with her three children and the suitcase-stroller. *Me, somewhere, in transit with a child.* I remembered. I had exactly the life I wanted. I still have it. Joy settles into you, too; its return can take time. I picked you up and carried you home from the bus stop.

There isn't a single detail about that day that did not delight you: folding the bus transfer ticket between your fingers, rushing into the theatre so as not to miss the trailers, the fact that you weren't big enough to keep the theatre's flip seat folded down. We watched *The Addams Family 2*; you decided that afternoon you wanted to dress up as Dracula for Halloween. "The *real* one," you said, referring to Bela Lugosi, and to this day I do not know how you learned that name. I painted your face white, combed your hair with gel, shadowed your eyes grey, drew lines of blood around your mouth with lipstick, the way Jamaica Kincaid once described doing for her young daughter at her own request. Her daughter wore an old hat of hers, an important, meaning-making object of her twenties. I used a ropey, golden, magnet-clasped necklace of the same significance to hold your cape together. You scared the hell out of your kindergarten classmates that year, and I loved you for it.

Children learn to categorize after experiencing each thing anew, yes, and while the need for this diminishes with age, those who care for them also get to relearn from witnessing this process. You witness joy and relearn it. You learn that the heart beats again. Or, more accurately, you return to the fact, however many times in your life you need to, that it never stopped to begin with.

RE: PART-TIME JOB

Hi Chantal,

No big deal, but I'd like to clear up something small. When I was an auditor, at City Hall, I was given permission to take six months off. To enable that, I worked about a year delivering for Swiss Chalet in the evening/night after my day job. The toughest part was when some called me "the chicken man." I was clandestine about this job as many at that time did not look kindly on this type of work.

I cancelled my plan and used those savings on a down payment for a townhouse, just before Mom and I married. When I was a teen in England, I also had a part-time job in a pub, but lasted only one day.

The reason for the above narrative is so Fa knows that when he is older. As he may also tell others I used to deliver pizza. Whilst I am not ashamed, believing all jobs have dignity, I want Fa to know my whole working life, and not just that one episode.

Hope you all have a restful evening and sleep well.
Love to all.

Dad

ANY VISITOR TO VALLARTA has seen El Caballito, a verdi-gris boy on a seahorse waving from the downtown shore-line. The bronze statue, commissioned of sculptor Rafael Zamarripa, was erected in 1968, the year my mother's family arrived. Shortly after its installation, a hurricane tore it from its stone base and carried it out to sea. The city installed a larger reproduction in 1976.

The original Caballito returned twice. It washed up in the late seventies and was reinstalled at Playa de los Muertos, past the foot of the boardwalk, the twin statues emphasizing the place Vallarta was becoming, had become. My mother, a teenage aunt by then, would strap her first niece into an umbrella stroller and walk her along the shoreline between the two statues.

In 2002, Hurricane Kenna pried the little boy on the seahorse from the stone base a second time. After its recovery this time, the city bolted it to a rock with steel rods.

For years my mother insisted she'd move back to Vallarta someday, but the summer after your brother was born she stopped talking about this.

TWO SUMMERS AFTER YOUR brother was born, we returned to Vallarta. All of us. I packed: swimming diapers, life jackets, rash guards, water shoes, sunscreen. As few clothes as possible. As few things as possible. Even edited down, there was still so much of us. Car seat, stroller, rolling suitcase, your two little backpacks full of modelling clay and colouring things. My mother rolled your brother along; your father held your hand. I dipped you both into the ocean and didn't flinch once.

We drove up the hill to the house with the wooden door. I lifted you up to knock.

HEY HONEY, CAN YOU go back downstairs with Mamá Rú? I just need to finish this last bit.

What are you doing, Mama?

I'm working, baby.

I just want to sit with you. Why's your computer up here?

Well . . . I'm writing. It's a bit noisy downstairs.

What are you writing about?

Us! Or about Mamá Rú and Pa too. And when you were born. And—

I'm in it?

Yes—please don't touch the charger! The cable is broken.

What do I do?

Well, there's parts from when you were very little and—

Like when I was a baby?

Yes! When you were born, and even before, and even after, like when—

Can I read it?

How about I read it to you?

Does it have pictures?

No, baby, it's not a picture book.

How does it start?

You know what? I don't know yet. But I think I know how it ends. Are you hungry for dinner?

Ma'rú made noodle soup.

Let's go.

EVERY HOME HAS ITS own morning song. The rustle of the cutlery drawer, the jumping jacks my father did in the basement, the weekend hum of the vacuum cleaner. I was most at peace lying in bed, listening to these things my parents did in the home they kept for us before I made myself known to the day. They were their uninterrupted selves; I had yet to become one.

These days, my children are the ones to wake my husband and me. The pace of their lives is still our clock. If I'm lucky, fifty years from now I'll recall the hurried rhythm of their feet bounding down the hallway, the click of the bedroom door. I'll be able to remember this crux in my life that felt at once like a sieve and a brick wall; like time collapsing in upon itself and expanding. A period when, as much as labour and label, motherhood constituted a form of time travel. They taught me this.

My children are too young to sleep in right now. But I know those years are coming. I sometimes think about what they will wake to, what my uninterrupted self will sound like then.

WORKS CITED AND FURTHER READING

Sibilla Aleramo, *A Woman*, translated by Rosalind Delmar,
    University of California Press, 1983.
Jazmina Barrera, *Linea Nigra*, translated by Christina
    MacSweeney, Two Lines Press, 2022.
Eula Biss, *On Immunity: An Inoculation*, Graywolf Press, 2014.
Dionne Brand, *A Map to the Door of No Return: Notes to
    Belonging*, Vintage Canada, 2002.
Angela Carter, *Wise Children*, Vintage Classics, 1992.
Marosia Castaldi, *The Hunger of Women*, translated by Jamie
    Richards, And Other Stories, 2023.
Ted Chiang, *Stories of Your Life and Others*, Tor Books, 2002.
Rachel Cusk, *Second Place*, Farrar, Straus & Giroux, 2021.
Joan Didion, *Blue Nights*, Alfred A. Knopf, 2011.
Elena Ferrante, *The Story of the Lost Child*, translated by Ann
    Goldstein, Europa Editions, 2015.
Rivka Galchen, *Little Labors*, New Directions, 2016.
Angela Garbes, *Essential Labor: Mothering as Social Change*,
    HarperCollins, 2022.

Alexandra Kimball, *The Seed: Infertility Is a Feminist Issue*, Coach House Books, 2019.

Jamaica Kincaid, *The Autobiography of My Mother*, Farrar, Straus & Giroux, 1996.

Jamaica Kincaid, *A Small Place*, Farrar, Straus & Giroux, 1988.

Jhumpa Lahiri, *In Other Words*, translated by Ann Goldstein, Alfred A. Knopf, 2016.

Ulrich Lehmann, *Tigersprung: Fashion in Modernity*, MIT Press, 2002.

Sarah Manguso, *Ongoingness: The End of a Diary*, Graywolf Press, 2015.

Lee Maracle, *Memory Serves: Oratories*, NeWest Press, 2015.

Cherrie Moraga, *Waiting in the Wings: Portrait of a Queer Motherhood*, Firebrand Books, 1997.

Maggie Nelson, *The Argonauts*, Graywolf Press, 2015.

Doireann Ní Ghríofa, *A Ghost in the Throat*, Biblioasis, 2021.

Sylvia Plath, *Collected Poems*, Faber & Faber, 2002.

Jacqueline Rose, *Mothers: An Essay on Love and Cruelty*, Farrar, Straus & Giroux, 2018.

Y-Dang Troeung, *Landbridge*, Alchemy by Knopf Canada, 2023.

D.J. Waldie, *Holy Land: A Suburban Memoir*, W.W. Norton & Company, 1996.

WITH THANKS

This book's second epigraph, spoken multiple times by Ursula Le Guin at lectures and eventually printed in an essay for the *New York Times* in 1989, is more than just demonstrative. It structurally describes the making of this book, as it does so many others written by new mothers, whether those books are explicitly about the act of mothering or not.

The weeks I spent starting the manuscript were supported by the Ontario Arts Council and the Toronto Arts Council. The time I spent taping it back together and scraping it down, condensing it, over more years than I expected to, was made possible by the people I wrote about, who cared for my children while I wrote. Often in the same home, on the same floor, sometimes in the same room. How rich our lives are that there are more who have done so during this time: Diane and Rudy Cappelletto, Winnie

Berhane. My ability to finish this book while working full-time would not have existed without the help of Maureen Halushak.

To Denise Balkissoon, Emily Keeler, and Eve Tobolka, who read early versions of this work: thank you for your generosity and your friendship, an endless joy. To Stephanie Sinclair: thank you for believing in this book.

I have been in some form of conversation or other with Haley Cullingham about what this book turned out to be for almost ten years. I am grateful always for her ear, her eye, and her faith in me.

I have been in some form of back-and-forth with Robb Cappelletto about what it means to live well for more than half my life. If I'm lucky, we will live this out with our children for the rest of it, however long that turns out to be.

To my father, who wanted me to write. To my mother, who wrote my life before me.

ABOUT THE AUTHOR

CHANTAL BRAGANZA is a writer and editor living in Toronto. She is currently a senior editor at Chatelaine. Her work has appeared in the *New York Times Magazine*, Hazlitt, The Hairpin, *the Globe and Mail*, *Toronto Life*, *Fashion Magazine*, and *Maisonneuve*, among others.